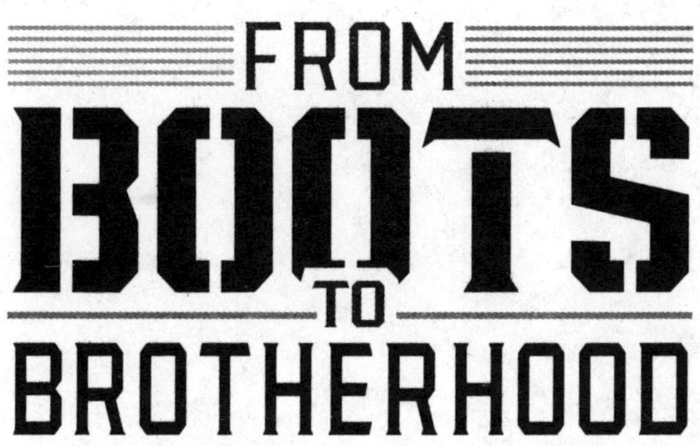

Cadets, Camaraderie and Chronicles

Cadets, Camaraderie and Chronicles

Shivam Sharma

Title: From Boots to Brotherhood:
Cadets, Camaraderie and Chronicles
Author: Shivam Sharma

ISBN: 978-93-49042-08-7

Published by:
JGS Enterprises Pvt Ltd
Imprint: The Browser | Fauji Days

Publisher's Address:
SCO 14-15, FF, Sector 8-C, Chandigarh 160 009

Website: thebrowser.org
Email: service@thebrowser.org

Publishers & Booksellers

Oral History & Military Publishing

To Mumma, Papa, and my Genie,
my constant support and strength.
Love you!

Contents

Term II: The Glory

Prologue

The state of Punjab has a long-standing tradition of producing brave soldiers who have been defending the nation for centuries.

It is the land where courage flows as freely as the five rivers. From the legendary army of Maharaja Ranjit Singh, the *Sher-e-Punjab*, to the fearless soldiers of the Sikh Regiment, their valour was immortalised in various battles like the one at Saragarhi, where twenty-one brave men stood against thousands and in modern conflicts such as the Kargil War, where Punjabi soldiers fought with unwavering bravery to protect the nation's honour.

To keep this legacy alive, Maharaja Ranjit Singh Armed Forces Preparatory Institute (MRSAFPI) was set up by the Government of Punjab, led by the then Chief Minister Sardar Parkash Singh Badal, along with the Institute's founding director, Major General BS Grewal, VSM. AFPI was envisioned as a breeding ground for the next generation of officers, ensuring that Punjab's proud tradition of service and sacrifice towards the nation continues. The Institute does not just train young boys for the Armed Forces; it moulds them into leaders and instils discipline and honour that runs deep in the veins of the men of Punjab.

AFPI, often termed a 'mini-NDA', has consistently proven its mettle as a cradle of defence excellence. Its cadets have not only excelled at the National Defence Academy (NDA) but have also earned places in the Indian Military Academy, Officers Training Academy, Air Force Academy, and Naval Academy. With over 200 cadets joining these prestigious institutions to date and more than 140 officers commissioned into the Armed Forces, AFPI's legacy speaks volumes. AFPIans have not only joined the various institutions but have made their name in the service ahead, from earning CDS commendation cards to excelling in various activities, solidifying the Institute's reputation as a hub of excellence.

This book captures not just the honour and determination of AFPI cadets but also the memories and bonds that define their journey. Late-night discussions, pranks, struggles, and laughter—all come together to narrate the story of ***The Titans of the Twelfth,*** celebrating two unforgettable years of pride, camaraderie, and the promise of service to the nation.

However, some stories, the truly unforgettable ones, cannot be fully shared. They remain part of the secret treasure of AFPI. To truly understand them, you must be part of it—experience it firsthand—and earn those stories for yourself.

TERM I

THE GRIND

For AFPI & all AFPIans.
Long Live AFPI!

46 Boys

Mai hi aaj se aap sab ka mather-father hu
—Warden Sahab

Pushing through the gruelling written examination, the nerve-wracking interview, and the exhaustive medical checks, there we stood—46 wide-eyed BOYS, ready to embrace a brand new life. As we gathered at the gates of the Academy, excitement mingled with a hint of anxiety. This was it; our journey was about to begin. The previous director had retired, and we were now under the watchful eye of the interim director, Air Commodore Sathe. Who was he, the new commander of our fate? More importantly, would he be the type to make us do 100 push-ups for just breathing too loudly? Too many questions were fighting in our minds about the time that lay ahead of us.

As our parents hugged us goodbye, tears mingled with pride and promises of 'we'll see you soon'. Little did they know, the promises would quickly turn into daily calls about lost socks and endless requests for homemade food parcels. They headed home, leaving us to fend for ourselves in this new, strange world.

We were allotted our squadrons, rooms, and the unique cadet numbers that would become our identity during this time. Some cadets even joked about tattooing their cadet numbers on their arms just in case they forgot after one too many push-up sessions.

The welcome ceremony included a spirited lecture from the warden, lasting a full hour, about what AFPI actually is and what was expected of us. As he rambled on, our minds began to wander. One cadet even dozed off mid-lecture, earning himself the nickname 'Kumbhkaran' to be retained throughout the two years. When he jolted awake, he accidentally responded, 'Yes, sir!' to a question that wasn't directed at him—let's just say, the next day, he became quite familiar with the Academy grounds during his extra nap time.

After the warden's lecture, we were told to set up our rooms and unpack our baggage. Everyone headed back, wrestling with their luggage, which somehow now felt heavier than it had during the journey here. Some cadets discovered that their neatly packed bags had mysteriously transformed into chaotic bundles—one guy even pulled out a pair of socks from his toothpaste holder. But just as we started settling in, a loud alarm blared through the corridors, echoing like a fire drill on steroids.

For a second, we all froze—some guys even ducked under their beds, convinced the Academy was under attack. But then it hit us: the hooter. We'd been briefed about this during the lecture—any time we hear that sound, we must report immediately near the stage. Chaos turned into panic-mode efficiency, and within minutes, we were assembled outside, looking like a bunch of misfit soldiers trying to form straight lines.

This time, the warden's mission was to introduce us to the mighty Academy appointments. First up was the Battalion Cadet Captain, BCC Kalia. Never mind the odd nickname; this guy looked like he'd walked straight out of an action movie, muscles bulging like they had their own workout routine. If intimidation was a skill, he'd mastered it to perfection.

Next was the BCA—the Battalion Cadet Adjutant. With his gaunt face and sunken eyes, he looked more like he'd just recovered from a long illness than someone ready to command a battalion. But his voice? It boomed like thunder every time he barked out instructions. And then came the three SCCs (Squadron Cadet Captains) for each of the squadrons—Alpha, Bravo, and Charlie, along with their CSMs (Cadet Sergeant Majors) and CQMS (Cadet Quarter Master Sergeants). They all seemed like they had stepped out of a boot camp commercial, each of them holding an expression that said, 'I can make you do push-ups until you forget how to count.'

After the introductions, we were sent back to our rooms, where we quickly realised this place wasn't going to be just another summer camp. Then, at precisely 8 p.m., the hooter blared again—this time, signalling dinner. And let me tell you, the moment that sound hit our ears, it was as if someone had fired a starter pistol at a track meet. All of us launched ourselves towards the mess hall, sprinting like our lives depended on it. When we entered the mess, we were pleasantly surprised—the food was laid out neatly, looking like a buffet from a five-star hotel. The aroma was enough to make us feel like kings for the night.

As we hurriedly settled down at the tables, just as we were about to dig in, one of the mess staff gave us a stern warning: 'The last table row is reserved for the seniors—no juniors allowed.' We quickly adjusted, squeezing into the remaining tables, eager to enjoy the meal.

The food was genuinely good—much better than the horror stories I'd heard about hostel mess food. As we ate, the chatter started naturally. We couldn't help but share our excitement and joke about the first day's events. But just as the volume rose, the door to the mess swung open again, and in walked a senior. He glared at us like we'd just committed a crime against the Academy. Without missing a beat, he bellowed, '*Oye* juniors! Can't you stay under your boots? It's just been a day, and you're already shouting in the mess! Don't you have any decency?'

His voice echoed through the mess hall like a thunderclap. We froze, spoons halfway to our mouths, feeling like we'd just been caught cheating in an exam. It was as if the air itself had been scolded into silence. One guy next to me muttered under his breath, 'Man, I didn't know even talking was a crime here.' We all stifled our laughter, afraid that even a chuckle would result in us being asked to do push-ups right there beside our dinner plates.

As soon as he left, we exchanged amused glances, pretending to zip our mouths shut while our hearts still beat a little faster from the scare.

◆◆◆

After dinner, we had about forty-five minutes to roam around before the next fall-in. It felt like a precious little pocket of freedom, and we all made the most of it. Some of us wandered around, taking in every corner of our new world—peeking into the gym, marvelling at the parade ground, or just breathing in the cool night air. Others grouped up in small clusters, swapping stories about our backgrounds and discussing everything from the written exam nightmares to which squadron had the best view from the cubicles.

It was during this time that some of the juniors, just barely twelve hours into the Academy, began to treat the seniors like they were living legends. You could spot them from a mile away like the sound of the universe, hanging around the seniors with an eager expression, nodding enthusiastically at every word as if the seniors were dispensing wisdom straight from the holy texts. They started offering to carry the seniors' water bottles, taking notes when they spoke, and nodding at every instruction like they'd just received a direct order from the Prime Minister himself.

One guy even managed to say, 'Sir, you're like a god to us!' with such sincerity that we had to bite our tongues to keep from laughing out loud. He then followed up by practically begging, 'Sir, please bless me with your success tips.' We half-expected him to fall at the senior's feet like a disciple awaiting enlightenment.

Meanwhile, the rest of us just exchanged amused glances, whispering, 'Well, he's clearly aiming for a "Best Junior" award... if that's even a thing!' It was all in good fun, though, and we secretly admired their enthusiasm, even if they did look like they were ready to polish boots with their own sleeves.

But soon enough, the hooter rang, cutting our banter short. Like clockwork, we all scrambled to gather near the designated area for the fall-in, still chuckling about our 'devoted disciples'. This time, we were slightly less confused, but the butterflies in our stomachs reminded us that this was just the beginning of many more such moments.

Picture this: We're standing there, fresh recruits in a sloppy line, trying to act like we know what's going on when the BCA standing tall on the stage yells, 'Battalion, *savdhan*!'—the command for attention. Most of us froze like deer caught in headlights, confused about whether to salute, stand still, or simply blink in unison. But then came the real surprise: our seniors standing behind us stomped their boots into the ground with such force that it felt like an earthquake drill. The sound was so loud that one of the cadets next to me nearly jumped out of his boots, convinced that he'd been struck by lightning.

The BCA then turned back and gave the report to the BCC Kalia, who looked like he was born for this moment. And with military precision, the BCC delivered the report to the warden, who nodded as if he was reviewing an Oscar-winning performance. As they marched in perfect sync, their boots hitting the ground like drumbeats, we couldn't help but be awed. It was as if we were watching a Broadway show with military choreography—Kalia & Company: The Marching Musical.

When the warden finally said '*vishram*' (at ease), we let out a collective sigh of relief, though most of us had no clue what was going on. He informed us that we'd be starting school the next morning at 7:30 a.m. and needed to report to the Physical Training (PT) ground at 5:30 a.m. sharp for our first session. The news was met with a mixture of groans and whispered prayers as we all silently wondered how we'd survive a day that started before the sun even had a chance to show itself.

As the warden commanded, 'Battalion, *savdhan!* Line *tod*!' all the seniors started marching back to their rooms. Just as the warden turned to leave, BCC called out, '*Oye* juniors! Report to your ODs! They'll help you understand everything.' I thought to myself, 'Great, let's get this over with,' and straightened my uniform as I headed to my OD's room.

◆◆◆

The Overstudies were referred to as ODs in short. Their main duty was to turn their *undy* (understudy) into a disciplined cadet. If any mistake was made by the *undy*, all the fingers were pointed at the OD. And trust me, when that happened, the OD knew what he had to do: prepare a session of punishment for his *undy* that would make even the most hardened junior sweat! All the ODs had their rooms next to their *undies*, which made for an entertaining neighbourhood.

As I entered room number 35, I said, 'Good evening, sir!' My OD made me sit in a chair, which felt more like a throne of judgment. He then launched into a lecture about the importance of greeting each and every staff member and senior, stressing that this was the most crucial duty. 'Break this rule, and you'll find yourself on the receiving end of some delightful punishments,' he warned, grinning like he'd just shared a secret about the world ending.

Then he introduced himself as Alex Pranav Chaudhary, the head boy of Shemrock, and boy, did his personality scream it! After an hour-long session, which felt more like a TED Talk on survival skills in the Academy, he wrapped it up with some golden advice: 'Walking in slippers? That's a luxury reserved for seniors. And you—' he pointed dramatically at me, 'you can't step out of your cubicle in civil clothes! You must be fully dressed, either in your PT gear or your mufti.'

He even squeezed a little introduction out of me, asking about my family and dreams, and I had to fight back laughter when I admitted that my biggest dream at the moment was to survive the first week without embarrassing myself too much. Finally, at 10:30 p.m., after what rather felt like an eternity, he sent me on my way, leaving me both amused and bewildered about what lay ahead.

◆◆◆

On the first night, many of us were in room number 41, the topmost room, one that no one wanted to visit, staring at the ceiling fan above, which creaked ominously like it had seen many generations of clueless cadets before us. Then Kumbhkaran whispered, 'If this fan falls, at least I'll get to go home early.' It broke the tension, and we all laughed—softly because we didn't want our seniors to catch us having fun on the first night. Just then, one junior raised his voice, breaking the tension. 'Guys, my OD was saying we're in our honeymoon period! You know, that lovely phase where no *ragda* (intense physical training) would be happening, and we're expected to learn all the rules within this week.'

A collective sigh of relief washed over us at the thought of a brief respite. But then he added, 'But if anyone pulls off an extraordinary skill that ends up being a massive mistake, that honeymoon period will be cancelled for that guy!' His dramatic delivery made everyone chuckle, reminding us that while we were supposed to be serious cadets, a little humour could go a long way in easing our nerves.

With that note hanging in the air, we all felt a bit more relaxed, the tension that had gripped us since we arrived slowly melting away. One by one, we left the room, ready to catch some sleep and recharge for the challenges that awaited us the next morning.

Game on, Cadets!

Daud ke gate pr!!!
—PTI Rajinder Sahab

A sharp rise at 5:30 a.m., the hooter blared like battle horns 'HOO-OOOOOOoooooooo!'—that shattered the stillness of dawn and jolted every cadet into immediate alertness. With a collective groan, we stumbled out of bed, knowing full well that the day had only just begun and the real test was yet to come. Lights flickered on in a frenzy, illuminating the chaos in every cubicle. In one corner, some OGs[1] were already decked out in their PT gear, looking sharp and disciplined. Meanwhile, a few of us were still grappling with the concept of 'getting ready'—in my case, a monumental struggle just to locate my PT shorts.

Despite the organised chaos, the PT ground started to fill up with cadets lined up in the three squadrons. Ten minutes passed, and it seemed some of us had decided that 'fashionably late' was the

1. OG (Original Gangster) – A slang term for someone who is highly respected, experienced, or a veteran in their field. In this context, it refers to seasoned individuals known for their discipline and leadership.

new trend. That's when the drill instructor's voice echoed through the air: 'Check your buddy!' Ah yes, the buddy system—a lifeline, a partner-in-crime, and the person responsible for everything, including ensuring you didn't starve if you got sick.

Without a second thought, five cadets, including yours truly, sprinted back to the cubicles like we were in a marathon. I charged up to the top floor, where Squadron Alpha resided. I knocked on the door, yelling, 'Buddy! GBR! Randhawa Sahab! Wake up!'

Out came my buddy, groggy and dishevelled, with sleepy eyes that could rival a raccoon's. He squinted and mumbled, '*Haan, ki hoya?'* I shot back, 'Fall in!' That startled him awake faster than a double espresso, and within ten seconds, he somehow transformed into a fully functioning human, ready to face the world.

By the time we both made it to the ground, the morning prayer was underway, and I could feel trouble brewing on the horizon. As expected, right after the prayer, the drill instructor growled, 'Start rolling!'

I stammered, 'Sir, I had to go and call him!' The drill instructor shot back, 'Buddy late? Your fate!' After a few rounds of rolling, we finally joined the rest of the parade, feeling like we'd just gone ten rounds with a heavyweight champ.

Then came THE man to take the report: the legendary Physical Training Instructor (PTI), Honorary Captain Rajinder Sahab. He stood there with an air of authority that made you want to salute and run at the same time. When the BCC gave him the report, he said '*vishram*', and launched into an introduction of himself and then of our drill instructor, Subedar Swaran Singh, a man with experience at NDA, OTA, and IMA and then about his own vast experience at the Academy and in hockey.

We all exchanged glances, wondering how these 'old-timers' were our trainers. I mean, did they come out of a time machine or something?

Then came the booming voice of the PTI, '*Daud ke gate par!'* and all the seniors snapped into action like a scene from a military movie. We, the juniors, quickly followed suit, shuffling into line with the grace of a herd of sheep trying to follow their shepherd.

Rajinder Sahab then called out, 'Juniors *aage!*' and just like that, he took command of us while the other PTI took command of one lot of the seniors, and the drill instructor managed the other lot who were already in their crisp drill uniforms in the adjacent ground. These seniors, marching in perfect synchronisation, executed their movements under the watchful eye of the drill instructor, their high voices ringing out with the discipline and fervour of seasoned soldiers.

Rajinder Sahab took off running, and within a couple of minutes, most of us were gasping for air, feeling like we'd just run a marathon. We'd underestimated the 'old man'—he was running faster than a cheetah on caffeine! But he stopped to give us a break, probably sensing our despair. After all, it was our first day, and he didn't want us to lose hope just yet. We managed to cover about three kilometres, and he announced, 'For a few days, we'll do 3 km and then switch to five!' A collective gasp arose; if this was three, what in the world would five look like? But then we saw the seniors entering the gates at the same time as us, the only difference being that we had run three while they had completed the whole 5 km.

Once we were back at the Academy, we lined up for some push-ups. The air was filled with the booming voice of the drill instructor as he shouted, 'Parade, *savdhan!* Parade, *samne se tej chal;* parade, *piche mud!*' It felt like we were caught in a military thriller where we had no idea what was happening but had to comply anyway. We were left awe-struck as the seniors, with equal energy, were executing the commands with absolute precision and high spirits, embodying the very essence of military life.

After our gruelling PT session, we were called back for another fall-in. The seniors stood in front and shouted, '*Nishchay Kar Apni!*' to which the rest of us responded in unison, '*Jeet Karoon!*' a dialogue that we hoped would summon some strength.

Next, we trudged over to our designated squadron area for more push-ups. There, our senior rallied us with a chant of 'Alpha! Alpha! Alpha!' with push-ups that felt like an eternity. This was followed by a relentless '*We Live, We Work, We Die for Alpha!*', the squadron motto showcasing the *josh* still left even after the gruelling PT session.

The same show unfolded for the other squadrons: Bravo shouted, 'Bravo! Bravo! Bravo!' with the fierce determination of a gladiator and Charlie's rallying cry, 'Be aware, Cheetahs here!' echoed in the air! Each squadron proudly proclaimed its identity as we struggled through our exercises, all while wondering how the seniors made it look so easy.

By this time, it was already 7:00 a.m., and our seniors had a tight schedule—they had just twenty minutes to get ready for school, while we newbies had a generous forty minutes, at least for the first week. After that, the tables would turn, alternating who had to make it up earlier. But even with those extra twenty minutes, we barely managed to scrape by. Imagine the scene: a mad dash of rookies trying to brush, bathe, gulp down breakfast, and get dressed, all while praying that the PTI didn't decide to drop by for a surprise check. Meanwhile, the seniors breezed through their routine, getting showered, dressed, and finishing breakfast with the precision of a Formula 1 pit stop. And there we were, still scrambling to find matching socks.

The warden gave us a pitying look and said, 'It's your first week, so I won't say anything... but you better learn fast.' The message was loud and clear: this extra time was a privilege, not a right, soon to be gone like our morning sleep.

◆◆◆

Now, the ultimate rule of mess was to stay silent, but who are we kidding? That's when 'Marcos', another coursemate of mine nicknamed after his dream to join the Naval Special Force, never the one to keep quiet, started chatting away, clearly not realising he was in a place where silence was sacred.

The PTI, hearing Marcos' chatter from across the mess hall, couldn't resist. With a smirk, he barked, 'You! Since you love to talk so much, how about you talk while balancing your chair on your head?' Without waiting for Marcos to protest, the PTI ordered,

'Pick it up, put it on your head, and give us ten rounds around the mess!' Marcos, looking like a confused statue with a chair wobbling on his head, had no choice but to comply. As he trudged along, we all kept a respectful silence, watching him march those rounds. It was clear—no one was above the rules.

◆◆◆

It was our first day at Shemrock, the hub of our academic studies, and let's just say the day didn't exactly start on a high note. We stumbled into school a good twenty minutes late—with half-tied shoes and praying that no teacher would spot us. The first thing that caught our attention was the massive sports ground, complete with a state-of-the-art arena. For a brief moment, we let ourselves dream—imagining future victories and trophies etched with our names. But that moment was short-lived because reality was waiting just beyond the gate.

The school building was a masterpiece. Fully furnished and with a sleek design, it looked more like a corporate office than a school. But then came the infamous one-foot-high L-shaped wall near the entrance—a feature so ridiculous it had no purpose other than making us wonder why it even existed. Crossing it felt like we were entering a fortress, albeit one designed to frustrate rather than impress.

The real kicker came when we stepped inside. The classrooms were located in an alley near the coordinator's office, a strategic position that felt less like a coincidence and more like a warning: 'We're watching you.' There were five dark classrooms nestled here, divided between two sections for each grade—11 'S' and 11 'H' for us, and just next door, our seniors in 12 'S' and 12 'H'.

Now, about these sections. Section S was the picture of calm—a bunch of meditative sages who, we joked, probably recited mantras before class. Section H was the exact opposite: a chaotic zoo of untamed, hyperactive monkeys. As luck would have it, this wasn't just a thing among us juniors; even our seniors carried the same vibe. And now, it was our turn to keep the legacy alive.

For a brief, fleeting moment, the air-conditioned classrooms gave us hope. The cool breeze from the vents and the sunlight streaming through the windows made us think, 'Hey, this might not be so bad'. But the school had other plans. One of the windows in the S-section was permanently sealed soon after, as if the staff couldn't bear the thought of us being too comfortable. Comfort, it seemed, was not part of the curriculum.

Classes started at 8:00 a.m. and dragged on till 12:30 p.m., a marathon that felt more like a slow march to doom. By the second period, most of us were fighting a losing battle against sleep. Some brave souls even attempted a quick nap, but they were swiftly brought back to reality with a 'gentle' (read: sharp) tap from the teachers. To their credit, the teachers were patient—well, most of the time. They knew we were still adjusting to this new routine, one that had our heads spinning faster than a merry-go-round.

Yet, for all its quirks, the school wasn't all bad. It had its charm—a kind of blend between discipline and chaos, elegance and mischief. Sure, the coordinator's ever-watchful presence felt like living under constant surveillance, and sure, the classrooms were positioned like jail cells near a warden's office. But we couldn't deny that the school was beautiful, that it had potential, and that, someday, we might even grow to like it. Or, at the very least, survive it.

At 12:30 p.m., the bus picked us up, and we were finally free for lunch. The seniors arrived a good half-hour after us and finished their lunch like machines while a few of us were still chewing through our last bites. Time management? Yeah, that was still on our list of things to learn—right after 'how to chew faster'.

It was 2:00 p.m. by now, and we had a short break until 3:00 p.m. And trust me, that hour was like gold. Everyone snored at the maximum volume possible, turning the rooms into a symphony of sleep. But all too soon, the dreaded hooter blared again, signalling the 3:00 p.m. study period. Our appointments rushed around, checking whether we were actually awake or just pretending. Those who were caught napping got wake-up calls that ranged from a senior's sweet and sarcastic 'Good morning, sunshine!' to a less gentle shake that jolted them upright.

After surviving the study session, we had our games period for an hour. The Academy offered every sport you could imagine: basketball, football, hockey, lawn tennis, volleyball, squash—you name it. But before we could even touch a ball, we had to complete rounds of the 600-metre ground as 'warm-up'. Seniors did five rounds like they were jogging through a park, while we were blessed with just two rounds—lucky us! We felt like we'd won the lottery, but deep down, we knew this mercy wouldn't last.

Everyone joined a sport of their choice, trying to impress both themselves and the seniors. I decided to give football a shot, just for the fun of it. And what do you know, I scored a goal... off my own leg! It was a glorious fluke, and I couldn't help but grin, especially when I saw the seniors' expressions—a mix of anger, shock, and reluctant approval.

The games session ended, and we gathered in the mess for refreshments, downing our snacks like we hadn't eaten in days. Then came another fall-in, followed by another study period, and finally, dinner. But tonight, the usual routine had a twist—something new and different awaited us. It was time for the first stay back, a mystery yet to be unravelled to us.

The Stay Back Shenanigans

Sahab, stay back karwale?
—The BCC

Reaching the stage as the hooter signalled the last fall-in of the day, we gathered near the stage, a sense of curiosity buzzing in the air. But tonight felt different. There was a vibe, and we couldn't ignore the mysterious smirks plastered on our seniors' faces. It wasn't long before we got our first hint—after the usual roll call when the warden typically declared 'Battalion, *savdhan,* line *tod*', he deviated from the script. Instead, he said, 'Battalion, *savdhan*, BCC to take charge.' Our hearts collectively skipped a beat.

As the warden turned to leave, the BCC roared, 'Battalion, *savdhan*!' His voice echoed like a thunderclap, and our nervous energy was palpable. Then he followed up with, 'SCCs, take charge!' At that moment, we knew something was up. The Bravo and Charlie squadrons immediately sprinted off towards their push-up areas, their seniors barking orders. But the Alpha Squadron? We just stood there frozen in our spots, knowing full well we weren't going anywhere. This was our territory.

Just then, the Alpha SCC, Sidhu, who looked young enough to pass as our own pesky younger brother, bellowed, '*Oye* Alpha, is everything alright?' We hesitated, staring at the ground like guilty kids caught sneaking extra dessert. Silence. And that's when we knew we were in trouble.

The silence was broken by the booming voice of the CSM, 'CAN'T YOU HEAR?' Suddenly, a few of us dared to respond with a faint 'Yes sir' but it was too late. He smirked, 'Bend!'—a command for the push-up position. In seconds, we dropped down, elbows trembling, arms shaking like leaves in the wind. It was push-up time, and the seniors watched with amusement as we tried to keep up, groaning and straining. Eventually, they let us up, but our legs felt like jelly. And that was only the warm-up.

'Welcome to your "honeymoon period",' Sidhu declared with a mischievous grin as if he had just delivered some twisted love letter. We glanced at each other, trying to act like we knew what this meant, but the reality was clear: our honeymoon wasn't about love—it was about tough love.

Next came the dreaded introductions. One by one, each of us had to stand up and share our names, our dreams, our family backgrounds—basically, our life stories under the stern gaze of our seniors. But just when we thought it was over, the atmosphere shifted. A sly grin crept onto one senior's face, and he leaned forward, rubbing his hands together. 'Alright, let's spice things up,' he said, eyes twinkling with mischief. 'Now, let's talk about your favourite "incognito stars" if you catch my drift.'

You could hear the collective gulp echoing through the squadron. One junior, clearly panicking, blurted out, 'Sir, I don't watch anything like that!' The seniors didn't buy it. 'Oh really? Then what do you do all night, recite poetry?' They laughed, and it felt like the temperature had gone up ten degrees.

The second guy tried the same excuse, but this time, the seniors were ready. 'So, you're the good boy, huh? Maybe we should call your home and ask them what you watch.' More laughter erupted, but nothing could prepare us for what came next. The third guy in line, clearly not one for half-measures, rattled off a list of twenty names—yes, TWENTY—within a matter of seconds, like he'd been practising since day one. The seniors just stared, jaws dropping. We, the rest of the juniors, could only stand there in shock, wondering how this guy knew so much.

By this point, there wasn't a single name left for the rest of us to offer up. So, the seniors switched gears, diving into a discussion of... well, positions. 'What's your favourite position, boys?' one senior asked, barely containing his laughter. Cue the nervous giggles and blushing faces as the rest of us fumbled through responses.

'Look at these shy little brides,' they mocked, slapping each other on the back. 'Didn't know we'd be getting so many newlyweds tonight!' They ribbed us, making us feel like the greenest of recruits, but deep down, it was all in good fun. And while it was definitely awkward, we couldn't help but laugh at ourselves, too.

Ah, the chaos that was happening in the Charlie Squadron that night was something else entirely. While Alpha was busy struggling through its awkward introductions and uncomfortable questions, the Charlie Squadron had ventured into... let's just say, uncharted territory. And I mean really uncharted. They had somehow turned their stay back into a full-blown competition of—wait for it—moaning. Yes, you heard that right. Moaning. A talent contest like no other, with the sole purpose of determining which junior could produce the most melodious 'sound effects'. The entire Charlie Squadron was in on it, cheering on like it was the finals of some ridiculous talent show.

And wouldn't you know it, they even crowned a winner. The best moaner among them received an award—well, sort of. His prize? A brand-new nickname: 'Moan'. Yup, the whole squadron decided that from then on, he would be called by that title. And, oh boy, he did not seem too thrilled about it. But hey, a nickname is a nickname, and in a military institution, you take what you get, no questions asked.

Now, while all of this madness was happening, I was still over in Alpha, blissfully unaware of the pandemonium that awaited me. That's when, as fate would have it, the Alpha SCC called me over and instructed, 'Go to Charlie Squadron and fetch the BCC. And hurry up, cadet!'

I nodded and casually started walking towards Charlie. Big mistake. It was one of those rookie errors that we never seem to learn from until it's too late. Just a few steps in, a senior's voice from behind me thundered, 'DON'T YOU KNOW THAT WHEN YOU'RE GIVEN AN ORDER, YOU RUN?!' His words cut through the air, and I knew instantly that I was in trouble. As punishment for my leisurely pace, I was given a different mode of travel: frog jumps all the way to the Charlie Squadron. And so there I was, hopping like a toad across the grounds, praying that no one else would see me in this ridiculous position.

By the time I reached Charlie's area, I was panting and trying to hide my embarrassment. But my suffering wasn't quite over yet. The Charlie seniors saw me coming, and their eyes lit up with devilish delight. One of them stepped forward and smirked, 'Do you have any moaning skills, cadet?'

I blinked, utterly confused. What on earth were they talking about? My mind raced, but I had no clue. 'Uh, no, sir, I don't even know what moaning is,' I replied, trying to keep my voice steady. My innocence must have amused them because they burst out laughing.

'Ha! So innocent, this one. Well, just so you know, we've given one of your coursemates a new nickname—"Moan". What do you think of that?' one senior asked, leaning closer as if he was letting me in on a big secret.

Now, I had no idea what this 'moaning' business was all about, but I figured I should try to be polite. So, in the most serious tone I could muster, I responded, 'That's a nice name, sir.' For a moment, the seniors just stared at me as if they couldn't believe their ears. And then, as if on cue, the entire Charlie Squadron erupted in laughter—real, belly-aching, tears-streaming-down-their-faces laughter.

At that moment, the BCC stepped forward, barely able to keep a straight face. He asked, 'Do you even know what "moan" means?'

My mind drew a blank, but then suddenly, I thought of the most logical explanation I could come up with. 'Sir, I think his real name might be Mohan, so maybe that's why you all call him "Moan"?'

That was it. That was the line that broke the dam. The laughter that followed was so loud that I'm pretty sure the entire battalion could hear it from miles away. Seniors clutched their stomachs, some of them just controlling themselves from falling to the ground, completely unable to contain themselves. It was like I had just performed the stand-up routine of the century without even knowing it. Even the BCC had to turn away to hide his grin.

When they finally managed to catch their breath, one senior, still wiping away tears of laughter, said, 'Alright, kid, I'll give you two months to learn what it is and the art of moaning. Let's see how you do.' I had no idea why he thought this was a challenge worth setting, but I stood at attention and gave the only answer that made sense. 'Yes, sir!' I declared as if I'd just been given the mission of my life.

But inside, my brain was doing somersaults. What in the world did I just sign up for? Was this some kind of special skill I was supposed to master? I had no idea. But at that point, I figured it couldn't be that important, and maybe—just maybe—the seniors would forget about it.

After what felt like an eternity, they finally called 'line *tod*', dismissing us for the night. I limped back to my room, feeling a mixture of relief and confusion. As I stumbled in, still trying to process everything, a bunch of my coursemates rushed over to me. They were all grinning, barely able to hold back their laughter as they clapped me on the back.

'Dude, do you even know what "moaning" is?' one of them asked, trying to hold back a giggle. 'Uh... no?' I replied, genuinely clueless. And that's when they finally explained what I had unwittingly gotten myself into. My face must have turned fifty shades of red as they filled me in, and I realised just how much of a fool I had made of myself.

And so there I was, with two months on the clock to figure out the art of moaning—whatever that meant—and a new sense of dread settling in. But honestly, as embarrassing as it was, I couldn't help but laugh at myself, too. After all, when you're a junior in a place like this, you learn to take it all in stride—frog jumps, ridiculous nicknames, and all.

That first stay back was a whirlwind—half torture, half hilarity. We stumbled back to our bunks that night, muscles aching, egos bruised, and cheeks sore from laughing. And as we drifted off to sleep, one thought lingered in our minds: we'd definitely remember this night, even if we couldn't feel our arms in the morning.

The Birth of the Titans

Sbse ghatiya course hai aaj tak ka – vary vad course
—Warden Sahab

At the crack of dawn, the new academic session brought with it a storm of change that swept through the Academy. With it came a new leader at the helm—a stern yet charismatic man, Major General Chauhan. His reputation preceded him. They said he had a way of spotting trouble like a hawk from a mile away, and if you made it onto his radar, you'd better pray. But for us cadets, this change meant only one thing: new rules, new energy, and a fresh set of challenges.

Our first encounter with the general was during one of those morning musters. He stood tall on the stage, eyes scanning over us like a drill sergeant measuring the mettle of his troops. As he spoke, his voice boomed through the Academy grounds with the kind of authority that made even the wind pause to listen.

'Welcome, cadets, to a new chapter of your journey,' he began, his gaze sharp and unwavering. 'Believe you me, here, you are not just individuals—you are part of a unit, a team, a family. Unity is not just a word; it's your survival.'

We all stood in formation, nodding like eager little soldiers, our faces set in serious expressions as if we really understood. But behind those facades, each of us was dealing with our own inner chaos. And oh, if only the new director knew what a mess lay beneath that disciplined exterior! Because, despite our perfectly lined-up rows and synchronised salutes, a storm was brewing just beneath the surface—a storm that would soon break the 'Titan' course in two.

It had been two weeks since we first set foot in the Academy, and by now, we'd figured out how things worked. The endless PT sessions, the constant challenges from seniors, and the rhythm of Academy life were becoming familiar. But the most important lesson our seniors drilled into us was about the squadron spirit. To us, the squadron was not just a group of cadets—it was our family, identity, and pride. Alpha, Bravo, and Charlie were more than just names. Each came with a legacy, and it was our job to either uphold it or redefine it.

Bravo had been the reigning champion for the past 11 years, a streak that they were fiercely proud of. Charlie was the new kid on the block, trying to find its footing. But it was Alpha, my squadron, that was determined to break Bravo's dominance. Our seniors made sure we knew that this was our year to rise. 'We'll change history,' they'd say, 'and you cadets will be the ones to do it.'

One Saturday morning, the cadets gathered in the mess for breakfast, catching up after a gruelling PT session. As we wolfed down our plates of food, the conversation turned toward the squadrons—Alpha and Bravo in particular. 'Tatyaal'—who earned his own nickname when the warden couldn't pronounce Tayal—always the loud one, got the ball rolling with a provocative statement, 'This year, we'll end Bravo's streak. Alpha is going to make history.'

'Bakra', who was known for his peculiar style of running like a goat, wasn't one to stay quiet. 'End our streak? You guys can barely handle the stairs without panting! Bravo is going to win again—just like we have for 11 years straight,' he shot back, his voice dripping with pride.

Tatyaal's face turned red, and he leaned across the table, his voice dangerously low, 'Your seniors' victories aren't your victories, Bakra. We'll beat you fair and square. You're just riding on their coattails.'

Bakra glared at Tatyaal, 'Our seniors were legends, not some wannabes like you. They knew the real meaning of squadron spirit. Do you think you can match up to them? In your dreams!'

The mess fell silent as the tension between Tatyaal and Bakra grew. Even the usually chatty Charlie cadets stopped talking, sensing the heat between the two. But no one dared to escalate things further—not in front of the mess staff and the ever-watchful eyes of the seniors who were overseeing breakfast.

But while we kept our voices down, the tension boiled over the next few days. In the classroom, the division between Alpha and Bravo became impossible to ignore. Alpha cadets sat together, discussing strategies to prove our worth, while Bravo cadets huddled separately, exchanging stories about their seniors' past victories. Even during lectures, there were glares, muttered insults, and competitive jibes thrown back and forth between the two sides.

Then came the real breaking point. The first BPT test. After an exhausting round of running, push-ups, and all the rigorous activities, it was time for the final challenge: the hundred-metre sprint. It was a test of speed and endurance, but more than that, it was a test of our squadrons' pride. The cadets were lined up in groups of ten, each ready to prove themselves on the track.

As the groups lined up, the remaining cadets sat on the side, cheering for their respective squadron mates. But what began as harmless cheering quickly turned into something much more intense. Alpha cadets shouted words of encouragement to their runners but also couldn't resist throwing in some jabs towards the Bravo cadets.

'Run like you mean it; don't let Balli show you how it's done!' an Alpha cadet yelled, loud enough for everyone to hear, a smirk playing on his face.

The Bravo cadets weren't about to take it quietly. 'We'll see if you can keep up, Alpha! Maybe you should call for backup!' one shot back, his voice dripping with mockery.

As each group of ten ran their hundred metres, the comments from the side-lines grew bolder, louder, and much more pointed.

The cadets were no longer just cheering—they were mocking each other's performances, calling out weaknesses, and taking cheap shots that hit below the belt.

'That's the best you've got, Alpha? Even your past would be ashamed to see this!' a Bravo cadet shouted, his voice laced with laughter.

Not to be outdone, an Alpha cadet shot back, 'At least we're not living in our seniors' shadows! You "Braves" have been jumping behind them!'

The comments became sharper, and the atmosphere on the field grew more charged. Some cadets exchanged glares that hinted at something deeper than just competitive spirit. The seniors watching from the sides grew visibly uncomfortable, but they knew that in front of the staff, they were no one to make a mark. But it wasn't until the director, who had been observing quietly from a distance, finally stepped in.

'Enough!' His voice cut through the air like a whip, silencing every cadet on the field. The director, a man known for his stern discipline, walked towards the track, his expression thunderous. The seniors, who had hoped to manage the situation themselves, quickly stood at attention, giving way to the director's approach.

'I have seen and heard enough of this disgraceful behaviour. Do you think this is how we conduct ourselves in the Academy? Passing cheap remarks and trying to bring each other down?' His eyes swept across the field, landing on both Alpha and Bravo cadets, who now looked down, avoiding his gaze.

'This test isn't about proving who can shout the loudest or make the rudest comment. It's about pushing yourselves, working as a team, and showing the squadron spirit that your seniors have been talking about since you arrived. You have taken the name of "squadron spirit" and twisted it into an excuse for hostility.'

He paused, letting the silence sink in, the weight of his words heavy on our shoulders. 'Your seniors built a legacy—not with insults, but with hard work, discipline, and unity. When they spoke of competition, they meant pushing each other to be better, not tearing each other down with disrespect. Do you think you're upholding tradition? You're tarnishing it.'

The cadets stood rigid, feeling the sting of his words. The Alpha and Bravo rivalry that had driven them to this point now seemed small in the face of the director's disappointment.

'And as for those of you who think that this behaviour will go unpunished, BELIEVE YOU ME. All of you—Alpha, Bravo, and even the silent spectators from Charlie—will join me for a round of *ragda*. Maybe then you'll understand what it means to work together instead of against each other.'

The announcement sent a ripple through the cadets. There were a few low groans, but nobody dared to speak up. The *ragda* was brutal—push-ups, squats, and sprints that left us gasping for air. Yet, as we pushed through the pain together, the bitterness began to fade, replaced by a shared sense of struggle. The insults from earlier felt distant and foolish in the face of the director's harsh lesson.

During this session, we were also introduced to new words we had never heard before, like *makra*—the stage where a person is fit enough to jump into action but pretends to know nothing—a master of camouflage in the world of cluelessness! Some of us immediately labelled ourselves as 'expert *makras*' in the art of playing dumb whenever possible. It was a handy skill, especially when tasked with some punishment.

After what felt like an eternity, the director finally called us to a halt. 'Remember this day,' he said, his tone softer now, though still firm. 'Remember that your squadrons are only as strong as the respect you show each other. Without that, you're not a team—you're just a group of cadets fighting for nothing.'

He turned and walked away, leaving us with our thoughts. The field was quiet, except for our heavy breaths. Slowly, as we caught our breath and the reality of what had just happened settled in, the Alpha and Bravo cadets exchanged looks—not of anger, but of understanding. There was a long way to go, but the message had been received. The road to being the best wasn't about tearing each other down—it was about lifting the entire course together, and that was the day the TITANS were truly born.

Rain and Sweat

'Aye aye aye... kahan ja raha hai, kahan ja raha hai?!'
—*PTI Rajinder Sahab*

Morning air hung heavily as PT loomed ahead—something everyone dreaded. Waking up before the sun, lacing up heavy boots, and heading out for a long run, push-ups, and every imaginable exercise. It wasn't exactly the best way to start the day. So, whenever it was time for drills, most of us breathed a sigh of relief. Drills meant less running and more stamping feet, shouting commands, and letting our voices echo across the parade ground. But, if I'm honest, drills never felt like my thing. I preferred the feel of the cool air hitting my face during a five-kilometre run. My drill skills, well, let's just say they were a bit... lacking.

One morning, I was about to find out just how lacking they were. The drill instructor bellowed out his command, 'Parade, *savdhan! Samne se tez chal!*' Everyone was moving in sync, a rhythm that could only come from hundreds of boots hitting the ground together. But then came the fateful order, '*Dahine mud!*' and while everyone else turned right, I turned left.

'*Thum!*' the instructor shouted, halting the parade. He stormed over to me with a look that made my heart skip a beat, his hands wide open, ready for what he called a 'sandwich slap'. And sure enough, I was the tomato caught between those bread-like palms. That double slap felt like a special kind of discipline. From then on, I much preferred running 5 km over risking another slap during drill practice.

◆◆◆

But even running came with its twists and turns. One morning, something very unexpected happened. Our seniors had paused PT for a while due to their approaching NDA exam, which left us to handle all the PT sessions alone. Normally, if it rained early in the morning, we knew we'd be spared the long runs. We would hope for heavy clouds and a downpour, eagerly listening for the sound of raindrops. But as soon as 5:30 a.m. hit, the rain always seemed to miraculously stop, almost as if the Academy had made a deal with the weather gods.

And that day was no exception. We gathered for the morning fall-in, rain pelting the roofs and filling our hearts with hope for a cosy morning. But by the time we reached the ground, the rain had vanished, leaving the air thick with moisture. The PTI wasted no time and sent us off on a run. '*Daud ke* gate *pr!*' he shouted, and off we went. As if on cue, about 1 km in, the rain resumed, light but steady. But turning back wasn't an option, so we kept going, soaked to the bone, our boots squelching with every step.

After completing the full 5 km in the rain, we thought we were done. But instead of being dismissed, we were led straight to the gym, where things only got sweatier. With all of us packed inside, the gym quickly turned into a sauna, and the heat radiated off every one of us like a steam engine. Someone, desperate for air, dared to move towards the window, hoping to crack it open. But before he could even lift the latch, a sharp voice cut through the noise, '*Aye aye aye... kahan ja raha hai, kahan ja raha hai?!*' It was the PTI catching him in the act, and the poor guy retreated immediately, shoulders hunched in defeat.

And so, we carried on, sweat pouring down, smelling like a mix of old gym socks and stale bread. Every push-up felt like a battle, not just against gravity but against the heat and the smell. When the session finally ended, the relief was palpable. We stumbled out of the gym, gasping for fresh air like survivors of a battlefield.

We had one unofficial way of gauging how tough the PT session would be. The PTI usually arrived in his old, noisy car. The moment we heard that rusty engine groaning its way into the Academy grounds, we knew it was time to brace ourselves. But on rare mornings when his car didn't make that familiar sound, we knew that maybe, just maybe, we'd have an easier time. The other PTI would step in, guiding us through exercises with a bit more fun and a little less intensity.

That day, though, was anything but easy. As we dragged our tired bodies back to our barracks, soaking wet and sore, we learned that the morning muster wasn't just about PT or drills—it was about finding a rhythm together, rain or shine, slap or no slap. And despite all the hardships, we knew this was just another step to becoming something more.

◆◆◆

After the chaos of the PT session, we realised it was already 7:00 a.m., and panic hit us. We had barely any time to get ready, eat, and be in uniform for school. The rush was on. Some of us dove into the showers, and others made a beeline for breakfast. Meanwhile, there were the daily tasks of polishing boots, shaving for the non-Sikh cadets, and properly tying turbans for the Sikh cadets. The pressure to get ready at warp speed transformed the place into a battlefield of half-shaved faces, flying towels, and frantic boot polishing—survival of the fastest.

The real challenge, though, began when the hooter rang. This signalled the cadets to assemble near the bus for the school fall-in. A well-known rule at the Academy was that the squadron that finished assembling first got to sit first on the bus, while the last to assemble had to squeeze into whatever seats remained. Since there were always a few seats short, this daily ritual was like a mad race.

The Charlie Squadron, as usual, stood perfectly lined up as if they had been born-ready. They were the consistent winners, always first to assemble. But the real race was between Bravo and Alpha. For Alpha, the Achilles' heel was 'Rana', the perpetual latecomer. If our lives were a Bollywood movie, he'd be the brooding hero—the kind who always shows up fashionably late but somehow redeems himself with sheer brilliance in PT. Meanwhile, Bravo's challenge was 'Husan', our resident beauty king. Punctuality wasn't his strong suit—it was more of a graceful walk than a timely sprint.

But that day, against all odds, Rana arrived on time. His Alpha squadron mates looked like they had seen a ghost. Even the warden was stunned, probably considering whether he had woken up in an alternate reality. The Bravo Squadron's cadets, on the other hand, glanced nervously at Husan as he meticulously adjusted his perfectly folded uniform and polished his shoes to a mirror shine, as if he was preparing for a parade inspection rather than a fall-in.

With Rana present, 'Khassi', the Alpha Sergeant, immediately rushed over to the senior sergeant to give the report. Now, our senior sergeant or 'Guruji' (for he was the unofficial saviour of ours at all given times) was the golden boy of the Academy. He was practically the poster child, always topping the academic charts and excelling in PT sessions. Today, though, 'Balli', the Bravo Sergeant, looked defeated. He handed in his report last, his shoulders slumping with the realisation that his squad would be cramming into the bus tightly again. Balli earned his nickname because of his slim and trim frame, as straight and lean as a stick—hence, 'Balli'. He was also a constant gym brat, frequently flaunting his high-class pronunciations and proudly declaring, 'Actually!' before starting every sentence.

The warden, unable to resist, gave a speech praising Rana's timely arrival, a moment that made Alpha's cadets beam with pride. For the first time in nearly a month and a half, Alpha wasn't last, though Charlie, as usual, had already claimed the best seats. Bravo grudgingly accepted their fate, trailing in behind Alpha with Husan still smoothing out invisible creases in his uniform.

The rain and sweat from the morning weren't enough to drench our spirits for the day. As we returned from school in the afternoon, we realised that lunch was running a bit late. Our seniors had arrived before us, and the drill instructor announced that we had to wait until they finished eating. This meant the seniors would dine first, and a second hooter would signal our turn. But in the confusion, I, along with five others, completely forgot about this rule.

As the hooter rang, signalling lunch for the seniors, our group of six absent-mindedly walked into the mess. At first, everything seemed normal—until we noticed that the junior tables were empty, and a few seniors were still lining up. The realisation hit us like a shockwave. Panic flashed through our eyes, and we quickly tried to slip back outside, but it was too late. The drill instructor caught us red-handed, standing right there with his arms crossed.

'*Ab aa hi gaye ho to mat jao. Achhe se khana khao, phir dekhenge.*' His tone was sharp, and that '*dekhenge*' made my stomach drop. I knew instantly that we were in for it.

After a tense fifteen minutes, another hooter rang—this time for the juniors. As they flooded into the mess, their eyes zeroed in on us six, sitting awkwardly in the corner. They knew we had messed up big time. Faces turned red as whispers spread like wildfire. The drill instructor had explicitly warned that no one was to enter the mess until it was their turn, or the entire batch would face the consequences.

Lunch ended, and it was time for the study period. We knew that a storm was brewing. Everyone dove into their books, pretending to study, but our minds were racing with the thought that the instructor might burst in at any moment. Barely twenty minutes into the study period, a hooter rang unexpectedly. It wasn't time for games yet; there were still forty minutes left. But the sergeant's voice cut through the air like a knife: 'All juniors, fall in on the ground—NOW!'

We had no illusions—this was for us. As we rushed to the ground, the drill instructor wasted no time. 'Touch and back, football goalpost!' he grumbled. We sprinted, touching the post and racing back, barely catching our breath before we assembled. Once we were all gathered, he put us through a gruelling session of front rolls and spider walks. Some of the smarter cadets tried to slack off, but they were swiftly 'crowned' as Maharajas—an ironic title of punishment.

Hearing that word Maharaja, a memory hit me. Once, during a break back home, my mother had asked me, 'How's your life at the Academy?' Before I could answer, my dad, an Army man himself, chipped in sarcastically, '*Hamara bacha to hamesha Maharaja jaise rehta hoga, hai na?*' I just smiled and replied, 'Yes, Dad, I am the crowned king!' Thinking about it now, amidst all the *ragda*, that title felt like a joke.

Just when we thought we'd be rolling around forever, a hooter rang for the games period. The seniors gathered for their sports, and we were finally ordered to join them. Relief washed over us, but then the PTI threw in another twist: '*Paanch chakkar, go ho gaya.*'

We all knew what '*go ho gaya*' meant—five laps around the ground, each cadet sprinting individually with their best speed. Running in threes was a luxury, a comfort that we had grown used to. But today, our exhaustion from the earlier session made it tough to push through. Instead of breaking away to run individually as instructed, we all fell back into the habit of sticking together in threes, trying to conserve whatever little energy we had left.

After completing the five rounds, panting and heaving, we gathered in front of the PTI, hoping for a reprieve. But he wasn't going to let us off that easily. With a raised eyebrow, he said, 'I don't think you heard me properly. I said *go ho gaya,* not *tez chal.*' His words stung, but then a small smile crept onto his face.

'Okay, let's make a deal,' he said, almost playfully. 'Just one more round—this time, full speed. I'll hold back ten cadets; the rest can join the games.'

We gave it everything we had. The ground blurred beneath our feet as we sprinted, hoping not to be in that unlucky group. But the PTI had a twist up his sleeve—he didn't just hold back ten cadets; he held back twenty of us. Those twenty, including me, were given eighty push-ups, on his count, painfully slow, as a parting gift before he finally let us head off to join the rest for games.

As the games period came to an end, the final hooter echoed across the Academy grounds, signalling that it was time for evening snacks. We all rushed to the mess, our bodies still sore from the afternoon's punishment, but our spirits slightly lifted with the thought of some much-needed refreshment. After wolfing down our snacks, we moved out to the open grounds where free time began—whether for hitting the gym, polishing boots, or just catching a breather before the next round of routine.

A few of us gathered outside, right in front of the tuck shop—the famous 'Mall of AFPI'—which proudly offered a limited selection of pudding, juice, and the ultimate refreshment—*banta* (a chilled soda drink). It was time to unwind, to chat about the day's events, and to make sense of the day's madness. As we settled down, our coursemates surrounded us, and instead of the scolding we half-expected, they greeted us with laughter.

'Don't worry, you six. Today, we had it for you; tomorrow, you'll have it for us,' one of them said with a wink and a spank for all six of us. And as I looked around at their familiar faces, I knew those words held more truth than anything else. Today was our turn to take the heat, but this place had a way of sharing both burdens and laughs equally. It was one of those moments that reminded us all that no matter how tough the day got, we had each other's backs—and that made all the difference.

The Ripple Effect

Goli se kon marta hai? Heart attack se marte hai!

—PTI Rajinder Sahab

Yearning for success, we all valued our camaraderie and had learned the hard way that unity mattered more than anything. The lesson delivered by the director left a mark on all of us. But with time, the much-anticipated inter-squadron competitions began looming closer. The first event on the roster? Swimming. And let me tell you, if swimming were a way of life, I'd have been the guy constantly floundering, gasping for breath. Alongside me was Guruji, who wasn't much better in the pool, but he'd managed to balance his shortcomings with his solid academic and PT performance—something I was still struggling with.

However, swimming wasn't the only test we faced. Whenever we did something unacceptable in the pool, the punishment was swift and merciless: we were made to do front rolls on the cemented floor right next to the swimming pool. It felt like a rite of passage—or perhaps a cruel joke—each time we rolled over the hard surface, often leaving us sanded down and occasionally decorated with wet leaves as badges of honour. Nothing said 'you messed up' quite like a face full of foliage!

The first trial was a fifty-metre butterfly stroke, a test of strength and technique that felt more like a drowning attempt for me. Out of 46 cadets, fifteen of us failed miserably; some for incorrect strokes, and a few, like me, who couldn't even reach the twenty-five-metre mark before sinking like a stone. The director, with a stern but hopeful look, gave us ten more days to practice and announced a retest. It wasn't mandatory for all 46 of us to show up, but for the 15 of us who failed? It was sink or swim—literally.

The worst part about swimming was not the pool itself but the aftermath. After an hour-long session during the games period, our eyes would turn bloodshot, stinging like they'd been dipped in chilli powder. We looked like zombies emerging from the depths, craving one thing only—sleep. But, instead of resting, we had to drag ourselves back to the dorms and brace for the evening study period.

Our swimming instructor was a character in his own right. With his sardonic grin and knack for humour, he had a special talent for making examples out of the weakest swimmers. His favourite target? Our very own 'Panda'. Named for his round cheeks and cherubic face, Panda was a hit with the ladies outside the Academy for his boyish charm, but inside, he was the instructor's prime prey. The instructor never missed a chance to tease him, but Panda took it in stride, flashing a sheepish smile every time he was singled out.

The swimming instructor had another trick up his sleeve. Occasionally, he'd dive into the pool, much to our horror. When he entered the water, you knew it was going to be a rough day for somebody. He'd stealthily swim underwater, grab a cadet's leg, and tug them down just enough to give them a scare. The moment his hand wrapped around your ankle, you'd panic, flailing your arms like a windmill caught in a storm. It felt like the apocalypse was unfolding right there in the pool. And the instructor? He'd resurface, laughing like a man who'd just played the best prank of his life.

And those slaps on our bare backs? Oh man, it felt like he'd just branded his handprint into our skin. It wasn't painful, just oddly satisfying—like a strange tattoo of the summer.

One fateful day, our PTI decided to crank things up a notch for us strugglers. He looked us square in the eye and said, 'Alright, cadets, 100 m today. Let's see what you're made of.' Now, for someone like me, who could barely drag myself through 50 m, this felt like a death sentence. But then, he sweetened—or rather, soured—the deal with a threat that sent shivers down my spine: 'If you don't finish this, you'll be doing a handstand for the entire morning tomorrow. And don't think I'm kidding.'

As I stood on the edge of the pool, the thought of spending a whole morning inverted was enough to light a fire under me. I dove in, thrashing through the water like my life depended on it—because, honestly, it did. Somehow, I managed to reach seventy-five metres, my arms burning and legs cramping, but the PTI's voice in my head kept me going. And when I finally touched the edge of the pool, gasping for air, I realised that I had actually learned how to swim—or at least, how to survive.

The entire ordeal was exhausting, but when we finally crawled out of the pool, we found Panda chuckling. '*Bhai*, I thought you were going to end up as fish food out there,' he joked, patting my back. I shot him a look, half annoyed and half relieved, but the laugh was warranted.

Ten days of relentless practice later, the retest arrived. The atmosphere was tense, the water in the pool reflecting the anxiety and determination of every cadet. We dove in, each stroke fuelled by the desire to prove ourselves and avoid another round of embarrassment. It wasn't pretty—there were still flailing limbs, red eyes, and a few near-drownings. But somehow, we made it through.

As we lined up, dripping wet and exhausted, the director stood before us, a rare smile on his face. 'Well done, boys,' he declared. 'You've all cleared the test.' The words hit like a wave of relief. We exchanged tired but triumphant grins. We had managed to overcome our fears, our weaknesses, and the swimming pool that had once seemed like an ocean.

The Charlie Squadron took the top spot, with most of their men having cleared the test in the first go. Bravo followed as a close second. And then there was Alpha, my squadron, trailing in last—thanks to me and our lovely Guruji.

The seniors quickly learned that we both were feeling the sting of Alpha's loss. It was tough for us to accept that we hadn't delivered for our squadron. Just when we were wallowing in our misery, the BCA, also from Alpha, approached us with a grin that could brighten the gloomiest day. 'Cheer up, boys! Let's grab a treat. My treat!' he declared, and suddenly, the weight of disappointment felt a little lighter.

As we headed to the tuck shop, the BCA waved his hands like a magician, revealing his greatest trick. 'You see,' he began, 'this isn't the end of competitions. It's just one bump on the road. You'll have plenty of chances to prove yourselves.' With a wink, he added, 'And trust me, if I can make it through the final exam with a paper filled with doodles instead of answers, you can definitely swim through this!'

In that moment, I realised I had misjudged the man. He had far more wisdom—and humour—than I'd given him credit for. We left the tuck shop with full stomachs and lighter hearts, ready to tackle whatever challenges lay ahead. The BCA had not only picked up the tab but had also reminded us that this was just the beginning of our journey, and every setback was merely a setup for a great comeback.

We might not have become Olympic swimmers, but we sure learned to keep our heads above water—literally and metaphorically. And that day, we realised something about fear and teamwork. Fear can make you swim faster, but knowing that your coursemates are waiting with a smile and a pat on the back for you makes the water feel just a bit warmer.

◆◆◆

Finally, the long-awaited Sunday arrives, and it feels like the best day of our lives! With our seniors off taking their NDA examination, we bask in the glory of freedom, feeling like kings ruling our tiny kingdom of cabins. The warden? Nowhere in sight!

With the PVH computers wide open and begging for attention, we dive headfirst into our Sunday plans. We crank up the music, blasting it through the speakers like we're throwing a rave party in the library. Bodies start moving, arms flailing like windmills, and it quickly turns into a competition to see who can dance the worst. We're shaking off the tension from training, dancing like nobody's watching, but of course, everyone is watching, and they're loving it! 'Look at Moan! He's got the moves of a drunk giraffe!' someone hollers, and we lose it.

As the beats drop, we can't help but reminisce about our hilarious school-starting days, sharing the wildest stories that have us rolling on the floor. 'Hey, remember when "Sariya" (another super-thin cadet) tried to impress that girl from class 10?' one cadet starts, smirking. 'He was all suave until he tripped over his own feet! I swear, he looked like a deer caught in headlights!' Another cadet chimes in, 'He turned redder than a tomato! I thought he was going to explode!'

Then, Bakra gets thrown into the mix. 'Speaking of tripping, Bakra, remember when you were racing down the hallway and went straight into the wall? The sound echoed like a gunshot!' we shout, and Bakra, with a legendary excuse, shrugs, 'I was just testing the wall's strength!' Everyone bursts into laughter again.

And let's not forget Balli. 'Balli, you're so slim, you could slide under the door! Just a breeze could blow you away!' a cadet teases. 'Hey, at least I don't run like a goat like you, Bakra!' Balli shoots back, grinning, and the room erupts into another fit of laughter.

We can't help but giggle about 'Mau'. 'Why do you think our PTI named him that? What does it even mean?' someone asks, and Mau just shrugs with a sheepish smile and replies, 'It just means kitten.'

As the banter continued, we couldn't forget about our school Physical Education teacher. 'Every time our Academy bus pulls up to school, we enter singing, "Kiss me, close your eyes!" You should see his face! It's like he's trying to pass a kidney stone!' one cadet says, doing a spot-on impression of the teacher's unimpressed look. 'And you know he hates us!' another adds, cracking up.

Speaking of things that get under his skin, the L-shaped wall, or as we like to call it, the Great Wall of the School, has always been the ultimate shortcut to the entrance. I mean, as non-medical students, we get it—why take the long route when you can jump across the grass patch like a pro? Every time I do, I silently fist-bump myself and think, 'Hell yeah, Pythagoras, this is your moment to shine.' But of course, the discipline in-charge and Manoj Sir don't share my enthusiasm for Mr Pythagoras—they seem hell-bent on keeping his theorem off school grounds. And then there's the wall itself, this one-foot-tall structure that's always been there, but until now, it was just... well, there. No one really cared. But the moment we started using it as a shortcut, the school bouncer suddenly acted like we were trying to scale the Great Wall of China. 'What's up with that wall?' someone asks, bewildered. 'One foot is nothing!' We all burst out laughing, imitating the teacher's serious face like he'd just spotted a rare species of bird. It's like, who knew jumping over a wall could make you feel like a rebel? Pythagoras would be proud!

Now, let's not forget Moan. 'Remember when he decided to skip breakfast?' one cadet bursts out laughing. 'During the special morning assembly, he marches in like he owns the place and then faints straight to the left—right where the ultimate crush of the school is standing! I'm like, "Bro, you could've fallen to the right! You have a girl right there!"' The whole room is in stitches.

Then there's 'Mushki', who walks into the room, and it's like the smell of a dead rat hits us all. 'Every time he walks in, I have to hold my breath like I'm in a swimming contest! It's a disaster!' The thought of his legendary smell sends us into fits of laughter, and someone adds, 'I swear, I'd rather swim in a sewage tank!'

And 'Gyani', the 'knowledge king'—the ultimate double-meaning guru—gets his turn. 'What do you think about love, Gyani?' one cadet teases, prompting Gyani to launch into an exaggerated monologue about the complexities of relationships. 'It's all about double meanings, my friends! You've got to read between the lines!' Gyani proclaims dramatically, and we all look at him as if he's just delivered the next great novel.

'Dada', the boss, with a capital 'B', also makes us laugh. 'He walks in, and you can practically hear the "boss music" playing in the background! It's like he's got a personal DJ!' one cadet imitates, and everyone doubles over in laughter. 'And the staff thinks he's the reason for every drama in the Academy!' they all add.

As the sun sets, we realise that despite our silly antics and wild stories, we've created memories that will last a lifetime. We may not have the freedom of adults yet, but these moments of laughter and friendship are our treasures.

Just then, Dada stands up, raises his voice above the laughter, and announces, 'Guys! The seniors are back, and guess what? They're going for a straight one-week holiday! The week full of amusement we just had on Sunday is about to be followed by a week of even more fun! You better believe it's going to be the best week ever!'

The excitement is palpable! 'This is it, boys! No rules, no restrictions, just pure madness!' someone shouts. 'We can enjoy this week to the fullest! Let's make the most of it!' The energy in the room skyrockets as we all cheer in agreement, knowing this week will be one for the history books.

With that, we wrap up a perfect Sunday, our hearts full and laughter echoing through the halls of our Academy, ready to embrace a week of wild adventures and unforgettable memories. Who knew one day could hold so much joy?

The Wild Week

Tuhade godeya ne bhaar nhi jhelna!
—PTI Atma Sahab

Once unseen before, the first day our seniors left, the battalion stage—the sacred spot where only the BCC and the top brass stood—transformed into our own place. Juniors like us? We were never supposed to step on that stage, but for the first time in months, all of my coursemates stood on that hallowed ground, feeling like gods during the evening fall-in. We strutted around, puffing out our chests until, of course, the warden showed up. Like ants spotting a boot, we scrambled down just in time. The warden, with his usual stern face, warned, 'I want top-class discipline from you guys. It's just one course. I don't want any mistakes, or I'll make things real tough for you!' But, come on, what's life without a little fun?

That night, we planned something special: a game of hide-and-seek that spanned classrooms, cabins—basically, the whole Academy. The first seeker? Tatyaal. His job: to catch us hidden gems. If he called out the wrong name, he had to go back and start counting again. The game kicked off at 11 p.m., but let me tell you, it never ended. Tatyaal, bless his heart, only managed to catch a few of us. He even climbed onto the roof, checking behind every solar panel, but still, he couldn't catch everyone. Eventually, by 1 a.m., he gave up, went back to his room, and crashed—only to find four of us hiding there when he opened the door. He felt like such an idiot, muttering, 'Why didn't I check my own room first?'

Lucky for him, the next day was a holiday, so he dodged a bullet. Otherwise, those missing cadets might have taken their revenge with a little 'birthday special'.

◆◆◆

Speaking of birthdays, let me fill you in: at AFPI, birthdays aren't something you look forward to. Oh no, they're like a rite of passage—one that involves belts and shoes.

Our seniors had warned us about it early on, and after a couple of weeks, we witnessed our first birthday bash. The poor birthday boy got a few slaps and whacks—nothing too bad since our hands were untrained. But as time went on, the hits got stronger, and we got better at making each birthday, well... memorable. And Tatyaal? His birthday just had to come when the seniors weren't around.

Tatyaal knew he was a marked man that day. Everyone was out to find him. He'd been there for every other birthday, delivering the birthday slaps with enthusiasm, so this time, everyone wanted to get their payback. But more than hitting him, people were eager to get their hands on his unofficial buddy. Now, an unofficial buddy is like your sidekick—someone you hang out with, even when you already have an official buddy. But the rule was clear: you couldn't touch the buddy until you found the birthday boy.

Tatyaal, being the crafty guy he was, managed to hide all night. He snuck into room number 1, the then landline room, by leaving the window open when no one was around. When the guard locked the door at 11 p.m., Tatyaal slipped inside through the window, shut it, and lay low. No one found him that night. But when morning rolled around, word spread about his hiding spot, and he got his special treatment after school—belts and shoes galore. But don't worry; it's all part of the fun and the brotherhood here. After all, if you can't take a few hits, how will you handle the Army life?

The best part? The lights-out bash. All the lights are off, and the room becomes a battleground. Everyone throws whatever they can find—sometimes, it's just an old shoe, sometimes a pillow, and occasionally, a chair. But it's all in good spirits. 'You've got to toughen up, bro!' someone always yells, making it clear that it's all part of the AFPI way.

After the post-school birthday celebration, we all headed to lunch, eating with the satisfaction of a job well done. Tatyaal survived, and we all had a laugh about it later. But with four more days before the seniors returned, we knew this wild week was far from over.

As we sauntered into games that day, the atmosphere was electric. With no seniors in sight, it was every cadet for themselves. 'Yo, let's pick our teams!' someone shouted, excitement bubbling like a pot of boiling water. But just as we were about to dive into our glorious chaos, one poor soul yelled, 'Hey, remember we've got that trigonometry test tomorrow?'

A collective gasp filled the air. 'Bro, I was hit hard!' one guy cried, clutching his head like he was trying to avoid a hangover that hadn't even happened yet.

'Oh great, now we're all going to fail and end up as the dumbest cadets in history,' another chimed in, dramatically flopping onto the floor. 'Is there any way to bribe the Math gods?'

But in true cadet fashion, we laughed off the anxiety and went for games, determined to live our best lives.

As the day wore on, the warden looked like he was on high alert, eyeing us like we were a bunch of squirrels plotting a nut heist. 'Listen up, you lot! There better not be any mistakes today!' he barked. We all nodded as if we actually understood the gravity of that statement. Spoiler alert: we didn't.

◆◆◆

Night fell, and while most cadets hit the sack early, a brave few stayed up late, drowning in trigonometry formulas. Their brains were practically oozing sine and cosine, so they decided they needed some fresh air. 'Let's go to the rooftop!' someone exclaimed. 'Nothing like the great outdoors to refresh our minds!'

Well, apparently, the great outdoors weren't too thrilled about their presence because as they started their rooftop study session, they got so engrossed that they completely lost track of time. Suddenly, the warden caught them red-handed!

'Surprise, surprise!' he yelled, bursting onto the rooftop like a horror movie villain. The hooter blared at eleven-fifty, echoing through the night like an alarm clock from hell. 'What are you doing up here? Studying trigonometry? In your dreams!'

Sleepy-faced, our dreams halted mid-way by the midnight hooter. We rushed to the fall-in area, confusion etched on our faces, only to find a few of our friends looking like deer caught in headlights, sitting on the floor in the anteroom.

'What happened to you guys?' I asked, barely suppressing laughter.

'Dude, we were just trying to find "x"!' one of them replied, holding his head in shame.

And then the warden marched in, flanked by guards like he was leading a military parade. 'You think this is a joke?' he roared, his face getting redder by the second. He launched into a colourful tirade that could rival any stand-up comedian. 'I swear, if I hear one more giggle, I'm sending you all to the moon!'

After that, they were sent back to the rooms like misbehaving puppies. 'And don't think you're off the hook! You'll be running for two straight hours tomorrow morning,' the warden called out as they shuffled away.

The next morning, they showed up in full uniform, looking like they had just crawled out of a horror movie.

They were then subjected to the dreaded ET—Endurance Test—a punishment fit for the likes of us! It was a spectacle! We watched in awe as they performed ridiculous drills. 'Look at them doing Maharaja rolls like a bunch of overcooked noodles!' I joked with a friend.

Their punishment became a training montage worthy of a movie featuring them doing burpees and whatever else you could think of. 'Hey, at least we're getting fit!' one of them exclaimed, panting like a dog on a hot day.

After what felt like an eternity, those punished guys became the warden's favourites—seriously, they practically had fan clubs by the end of it. 'What's the secret to winning the warden's heart? Just get punished enough!' one of them joked.

And after all that chaos, one thing was crystal clear: the sales at the tuck shop went through the roof! Those poor guys fresh out of ET needed copious amounts of juice to recover from their daily dose of punishment. 'Tehla', the tuck shop owner and the real MVP of AFPI, was probably grinning ear to ear, counting his newfound riches.

Now, let me tell you more about Tehal Sir, whom we lovingly call Tehla.

When life in the Academy feels like it's falling apart and you're questioning every decision that led you here—there's one person who can fix it all. Tehal Sir. The Academy's very own Old Monk God.

This man wasn't just a part of the Academy; he was the Academy. Rumour had it that he'd been around longer than the oldest obstacle course. But what made him truly legendary wasn't his age or his wisdom—it was his undying love for one thing: *banta*.

Picture this: you're sitting by yourself, wallowing in self-pity after a particularly brutal inspection, when Tehal Sir appears out of nowhere, like a monk descending from the mountains. With his signature grin, he tilts his head and says, '*Putt, banta pina banta.*'

That's it. No greeting. No explanation. Just those magical words. If you try to dodge it, he'll hit you with his most charming, almost fatherly persuasion: '*Oye,* Academy *mein rehna hai toh banta toh pina padega.*' And suddenly, you're nodding along like he's just given you the secret to life.

The man's stories were legendary. He'd tell you tales of cadets who tried to bunk, who dared to argue with seniors, or who thought they could outrun the guard. And he didn't just tell you the stories—he acted them out. One moment, he'd imitate a panicked cadet scrambling under a bed, and the next, the guard shouting, '*Ruk jaa saale!*' The man should've been a Bollywood star.

Some said that Tehla Sir wasn't a real person but a spirit that embodied the soul of the Academy. Others claimed he was immortal and would outlive all of us. Whatever the truth, one thing was for sure: no matter how bad your day got, when Tehal Sir leaned in with that mischievous glint in his eye and said, '*Putt, banta pina banta*,' you knew everything was going to be okay.

◆◆◆

But that day was not one of the days when he was going to make it better for any of us. Just when we thought we had it rough, Tehla dropped the bombshell: 'From now on, the pudding will be forty-five rupees!'

'What? A five-rupee hike?' we exclaimed, clutching our wallets like they were made of glass. 'That extra five bucks is going to break us!'

But desperate times called for desperate measures. After four straight days of juice runs, the Trigonometry Terrors practically lived at the tuck shop. 'Who needs a birthday cake when you can have pudding?' one of the cadets quipped, trying to justify the sudden obsession with overpriced treats.

So, there we were, cadets turned juice junkies, drowning our sorrows and thirsts in the tuck shop. We may have been broke, but at least we had our puddings to keep us company!

With just two days left until our seniors returned, the anticipation was palpable. 'No more slippers in the squadron line!' one of us declared dramatically, as if announcing the end of an era. From now on, it was all about the game rig, PT rig, or the mufti for any squadron movements. We could practically taste the freedom!

We were on the brink of becoming seniors ourselves, knowing it wouldn't be long now. The seniors had already tackled their NDA exams and were gearing up for their 12th-grade practical and board exams. On top of that, they would be busy preparing for the Services Selection Board (SSB), making their return even more chaotic. But until then, we braced ourselves for the classic cadet suffering we all loved to hate.

Every day felt like a game of 'How Bad Can It Get?' and let's just say our mistakes seemed to fuel the fire. We were frightened that they wouldn't leave us alone for the epic act of getting ET—'If they find out, we're toast!' someone exclaimed, eyeing the corner as if expecting a senior to leap out at any moment. If only we had a dollar for every time we messed up! 'At this rate, I'm pretty sure our mistakes are on the curriculum,' another joked, trying to lighten the mood as we navigated the minefield of senior expectations.

But we knew one thing for sure: once they were back, it would be our turn to dish out the legendary torment! Until then, we were just counting down the hours, planning our glorious rise to senior status, and praying that our mistakes wouldn't haunt us too much in the process.

And if you're wondering what happened when the seniors returned, well, it wasn't exactly a grand homecoming. The lovable misfit cadets who had made their infamous mistakes were in for some special treatment. After all, one thing was certain: that dreaded ET was like a black mark on your record when it came to the inter-squadron championship.

For the first time, the lineup was amusingly different—there wasn't a single Apache in sight. Instead, it was all Bravo and Charlie! 'Look at us, the cream of the crop!' one Bravo cadet joked, gesturing to the crew like they were part of some elite club of error-prone heroes. 'Who knew failure could be so popular?'

The rest of us just shook our heads, chuckling at our predicament. It was a wild sight, but we couldn't help but admire how well the chaos unfolded. The once-feared seniors were back, and we knew they'd make sure the consequences of our actions were hilariously unforgettable.

Tabs, Tumbles, and Trouble

*Behench*d, mai kabhi gaali nhi deta!*
—*Unknown*

Under the sunlit skies, Shemrock, our legendary school, became the cradle of mischief and dreams. It was here we bent the rules, forged bonds, and built the foundation for all we couldn't do in the Academy.

The school had this uncanny ability to split us up into two entirely different worlds, all housed under the same roof. The 'S' section, the land of Chemistry, marched grimly into Uma Ma'am's classroom, where the air reeked of equations and sheer terror. Meanwhile, the 'H' section strolled into Maths class, a zone of organised chaos where solving problems was secondary to unravelling the mysteries of life itself.

Uma Ma'am didn't believe in 'warming up' or 'easing in'. The moment you sat down, she was already scribbling formulas on the board, her voice crisp and relentless: 'Write this down. Memorise it. Breathe it.' Within a minute, the 'S' section cadets were hunched over their desks, furiously copying pages of chemical reactions as if their lives depended on it. The class looked like a factory assembly line—constant, efficient, and utterly soul-crushing. Over in the 'H' section, however, it was a different story.

Our Maths teacher had this peculiar habit of starting with, 'Let's discuss permutation and combination,' but somehow ending up with, 'And that's why Napoleon lost the Battle of Waterloo.' It wasn't a lecture; it was a scenic road trip with no map, where the landmarks ranged from probability theories to geopolitical strategies. Half the time, we weren't sure whether we were learning about Math or attending a seminar on world affairs. But we nodded along enthusiastically, mostly to stay on his good side while secretly hoping we'd eventually circle back to something vaguely mathematical.

When the bell rang, the 'S' section spilt out into the corridor, looking like war survivors, their notebooks heavy with scribbles and their souls lighter from all the information drained out of them. They'd just endured fifty-five minutes of pure endurance training, their fingers stiff from relentless writing. In stark contrast, the 'H' section emerged like victorious philosophers—engaged, entertained, and, most importantly, refreshed. Sure, they didn't know how to calculate a factorial, but they could tell you why the US dominates the global economy.

But every now and then, even Uma Ma'am would crack. Like the time she was teaching us monosaccharides, and someone—probably one of the sleep-deprived souls in the front row—decided to rename it 'Sachkirat-arite' after Sachkirat, our coursemate. For a few glorious minutes, chemistry turned into a comedy roast, with everyone debating whether Sachkirat's 'chemical properties' made him reactive or inert. Uma Ma'am tried to maintain her stern demeanour, but when someone added, 'Ma'am, what's Sachkirat-arite's boiling point?' she lost it. The whole class erupted, and for a brief moment, Uma Ma'am became one of us. But just as quickly, she regained her composure, delivering her signature harsh statement: '*Beta, ismein aapka hi* loss *hai*,' before diving right back into her lecture.

And then there was the 'Melodiosa' debacle. During a singing competition, someone from the back suddenly blurted out, 'Ma'am, why aren't we allowed in *Monalisa*?' It didn't make sense, but it didn't matter—the name stuck. Uma Ma'am didn't even try to suppress her laughter that day, but like clockwork, the moment the laughter died down, she snapped back to her chemical equations as if the whole incident had been a mere blip in the space-time continuum.

Looking back, it was chaos in the most entertaining way. If we'd ever managed to personalise the periodic table, Chemistry could've been our forte. Sachkirat would've been 'Sacharite', Moan could've been a rare earth metal named 'Moanium', and Dada would undoubtedly be 'Dadamium'—highly reactive, prone to combustion, yet always somehow indestructible. But Uma Ma'am wasn't one to indulge in such nonsense for too long. Five seconds of fun was her limit. After that, it was back to the grind—Chemistry first, always. But the misery of the 'S' section didn't end here

The section was cursed—there's no other way to put it. If bad luck had a favourite child, it was us. The 'H' section had Sunil Sir as their Physical Education teacher. This man loved everything except to see the students studying. Every time the bell rang, the 'H' Section would be out on the field, playing cricket, football, or even something as random as tug-of-war, their physical education period converted into a games period. Their laughter echoed through the campus like a Bollywood picnic scene. Meanwhile us? We had Manoj Sir. The only game he believed in was mental gymnastics. Every games period turned into an extended lecture about discipline, life lessons, or some topic we didn't care about.

But fate wasn't done trolling us yet. One day, our section decided we'd had enough. Seeing the 'H' Section frolic outside was like being stuck in a zoo watching wild animals run free. So, a few of us mustered the courage to approach Seema Ma'am, the supreme authority of games schedules. With the sweetest fake smile we could muster, we asked if we, too, could go outside for games. But instead of granting our wish, she slammed the gates shut for everyone, even for the 'H' section.

When the 'H' Section found out, they looked at us like we'd committed a national crime. Their glares could've melted steel.

We knew we'd ruined their fun, but in our hearts, we convinced ourselves we'd done the right thing. 'After all, we're coursemates,' we told ourselves. 'If we can't play, neither can they!'

Misery, as they say, loves company.

But the lab periods were a different breed of chaos altogether. On lab days, we had to stay in school a whole extra hour, and naturally, our collective goal became to seek revenge. The Chemistry lab was where all the drama began. While Uma Ma'am passionately explained how a solution turned from blue to white or yellow to green, a few guys would slip to the back and start their own version of Breaking Bad.

One guy mixed HCl with soap just to see the bubbles, while another genius poured nitric acid on a piece of paper. Sometimes, their experiments resulted in test tubes breaking, or worse, smells so horrible that Uma Ma'am would pinch her nose and shout, 'LIVE (her accented version of the word "leave") the lab! *Abhi ke abhi* lab *chhodo*!' That was our cue to scatter like guilty cats.

Now, the Physics lab was supposed to be a place of precision and focus, but for the cadets, it was more of a playground of chaos. As soon as Mr Ashwani left the room for a 'five-minute break', the entire lab turned into a battlefield of ingenuity and mischief.

'Sosa' and Balli decided to test how far they could launch tiny paper balls using the spring balance. Balli stretched it to its maximum capacity, ignoring the warnings etched on the device. 'Bro, this thing can launch a satellite if we try hard enough,' he said, releasing the paper ball with a dramatic '3… 2… 1!' The ball soared across the room, hitting Mushki squarely on the forehead, who was busy aligning the laser beam of an optics experiment.

Mushki retaliated true to his style, grabbing the air blower meant for cleaning equipment and directing it toward Balli, who ducked behind a nearby lab stool. 'This is war!' Balli yelled, dragging Sosa into the fray.

On the other side, Gyani was busy trying to outwit the laws of physics. 'What if we used the pendulum bob as a wrecking ball?' he asked 'Lahsun', who grinned wickedly at the idea. Before anyone could intervene, they had tied the pendulum string to a heavy clamp stand and started swinging it. It almost knocked over the table holding the light interference apparatus.

Just then, Mr Ashwani re-entered the lab. The sight before him was nothing short of a disaster. 'What in the name of Newton is going on here?!' he thundered.

The room fell silent, but not before Gyani quipped, 'Sir, we were just testing the limits of physics!'

Mr Ashwani sighed, muttering something about how cadets and science experiments should never mix. 'Everyone, clean up this mess. And Gyani, stop trying to rewrite the laws of nature!'

As the cadets got back to tidying up, they couldn't help but grin at the chaos they had caused. It was just another day in the Physics lab—where fun and science collided spectacularly.

◆◆◆

Among all this drama and the looming shadow of the calendar, came the one thing nobody was eagerly anticipating—the half-yearly exams. For guys like me, this wasn't going to be a walk in the park. Nope, it was more like a trek through a forest without a map. We had to prepare to our absolute best, just to scrape through. Meanwhile, for guys like Guruji, this was their chance to shine—to earn that coveted torch on their chest, the badge of honour every cadet dreamt of. Even the ones who deep down knew they couldn't earn it still daydreamed about it, like imagining winning a cross country after barely jogging to the tuck shop.

As the exams kicked off, we thought—no, hoped—that PT would take a break. But no, the director had other ideas. He declared that PT would continue every single day except the day of the exam. Seriously? We thought we'd at least get some slack during exam prep holidays, but no, he wanted us to stay 'disciplined'. Even games were mandatory, right up until the day before an exam. That was supposed to help us unwind, but honestly, we were just unwinding into stress.

But some cadets were surprisingly clever about it. They'd attend every game session, somehow squeeze in study time, and still score the highest marks. Meanwhile, others took the 'preparation' route a bit too literally—they started making chits. Classic move, right? Some even got caught, and their complaints were sent straight to the director. But this time, instead of heavy punishment, they got a stern warning and were given a chance to retake the exam. And then there were the sneaky champs who never got caught—those guys strutted around like they'd won an Oscar for best performance in a spy movie.

As for me, well, I always felt like luck wasn't on my side. My friends would rub it in too, telling me stories like, 'There's this one teacher who lets you cross-check each other's sheets for half an hour at the end.' And I'd just sit there thinking, 'Bro, why don't I ever get teachers like that?'

During the exams, my seating arrangement was the perfect setup for disaster. In front of me was 'Doda', a guy with handwriting so messy you'd think it was a secret code, and behind me was Kirmada—yep, that's really the name given by us—a guy just like me, which meant I couldn't count on him for much either. Somehow, I barely scraped together a 69%, thanks to English and Physical Education bailing me out.

Meanwhile, there was my neighbour, my friend residing in the room right in front of mine, 'Singla'—this guy, let me tell you, was in a league of his own. Forget textbooks, he was living in a world of novels. And not once did I see him study for exams.

I'd look at him and remark, 'Man, stop reading all those fancy novels and study! You won't score anything like this!' But did he listen? Nope. He'd just nod, smile, and go back to whatever epic battle was happening in his latest book. I couldn't help but think, this guy is going to fail harder than I fail at keeping a plant alive.

Then came the half-yearly results, and to everyone's shock—Singla pulled out a glorious 84.6%. Wait, what?! How did he do that? The guy missed the torch by a hair's breadth! And here I was, trying to memorise every formula and equation like my life depended on it. Meanwhile, Singla didn't even look at his books.

It was like being next to a god—a god of selective memory. I swear, the guy could remember entire novels word for word but couldn't recall a single part from our own syllabus. And somehow, just remembered enough to pull a glorious score in exams. I just stood there, staring at his marks, feeling like I was the one who had missed the plot of the story.

After the exams, we had a director-teacher meeting in the MVH. All of us marched in, three at a time, like we were about to face a firing squad. Some of us, like Guruji, came out with smiles, while others walked out looking like they'd seen a ghost. But the mood didn't stay serious for long—there were too many funny moments. When my turn came, the director actually forgot I was there, thanks to the two guys next to me hogging all the attention with their endless praise or maybe putting them down. My report barely got started before the Chemistry teacher casually mentioned that I wasn't 'serious' in class. But the Math teacher? He threw in a few kind words to keep us from becoming the staff's next targets.

As the meeting wrapped up, we headed back to the games field, gossiping about who might get the torches. The next day, ten of our guys were awarded torches. Even the seniors were shocked to see such a big number. And, in a twist that nobody saw coming, the appointments were reshuffled—we had brand-new sergeants leading the charge. It felt like the Academy's version of a reality TV plot twist, with all the drama you'd expect!

◆◆◆

But as fate would have it, the newly crowned Alpha Sergeant couldn't hold onto his post for long. It all started the very day the new sergeants were announced. While we were busy figuring out how our lives were about to change, some of our seniors decided to give the Academy a taste of Bollywood and staged a daring night out. But they picked the wrong night—because on duty was Rana, not our always-late coursemate but the guard who had the vigilance of a hawk and the vibe of Maharana Pratap. Trust me, if you so much as sneezed out of line, Rana would appear out of nowhere like, 'Caught you, *beta*!'

And he sure caught them. Our seniors, planning to night out, instead ended up with 21 days of ET. It was like getting served a cheap buffet of punishment: no variety but plenty of quantity. To add more masala to this drama, the BCA got detabbed. It was a scene straight out of a suspense thriller—one moment, you're on top, and the next, you're handing over your rank to the new SCC Alpha. The SCC Alpha took over as BCA, the CSM of Alpha got bumped up to SCC Alpha, and our senior from room number 33 became the new CSM. It was a game of musical chairs but with ranks!

Our newly crowned Alpha Sergeant, still figuring out how to carry his new weight, decided to push his luck. One evening, he got caught at the Academy gate with a suspicious package: a choco-chip ice cream. When Rana, with his no-nonsense glare, asked, '*Kya hai ye?*' our sergeant tried to put on a straight face and said, '*Woh...* parents *ne kuch* fruits *bheje hain.*' The guard wasn't impressed. He opened the box, and boom, there it was—the most incriminating choco-chip ice cream in history.

And what happened to the ice cream? I wish I knew. Maybe it melted in the heat of interrogation, or maybe it ended up as an evening snack for Rana. But one thing was sure: our sergeant's time with the tab was over quicker than a bowl of Maggi. Detabbed, demoted, and off went the badge again. Enters the new Alpha Sergeant, Rana. With a mouthful of names, we all stuck to Rana. It was simple, catchy, and definitely more memorable when you had to yell his name across the field.

Now, if you think we were done making a mess of things, think again. Saturdays used to be our golden days—the only time we could order food from outside. But trust us to turn that privilege into a disaster. One such Saturday, the whole squad went all out, ordering pizzas, burgers, and everything greasy. Next day? Total lethargy. When Monday came, no one wanted to run. So, half the cadets suddenly developed 'stomach aches', with faces twisted in fake pain. But our PTI—who could smell lies better than cologne—knew what was up. He shut down the whole Saturday order program. By the next morning, a big fat notice was plastered on the board: 'No outside food orders allowed from now on.'

But as always, there was that one cadet, our freshly detabbed sergeant, who decided to test his luck again and ordered food anyway. Did he get away with it? Of course not. He and his partner in crime, Mushki, got a week-long suspension for their stunt. And to make their return even sweeter, they were gifted a fresh set of fourteen ETs. It was the Academy's way of saying, 'Welcome back, *bhai*. Missed you!'

And that's how our little privileges turned into permanent bans. One after another, we watched as ranks and rules were reshuffled like a deck of cards. All we could do was laugh (and groan) while we all knew—this was just another day in the life at the Academy.

◆◆◆

Soon enough, a mysterious message started circulating: 'Juniors, it's time to be labourers.' At first, we couldn't quite grasp what it meant, but it didn't take long before reality hit us—hard. One by one, our ODs approached us, dropping stacks of practical files on our laps. Maths, Chemistry, Physics—you name it, they handed it over. Their strategy was clear: Why waste their own energy when they had a fresh batch of eager juniors to do the heavy lifting?

It truly was 'Labour Month'. And while they chilled, we were up late, copying and compiling their work, our hands aching from writing all those derivations and diagrams. But I can't complain too much—my OD had my back more often than not. Whenever other seniors tried to offload their files onto me, he'd intervene, waving them off. But let's not romanticise it too much. He still made sure I was busy—the only difference was that I was now crafting files on his behalf instead of someone else's. A relief, but barely.

Then there was 'Bhoru', a fellow coursemate with an unforgettable nickname that made him the butt of our jokes. He earned the name, for he always made lame jokes that pulled out a laugh from no one except himself. He was the ultimate yes-man, never turning down a request from any senior, which meant that he ended up completing about twenty practical files. I once asked him, 'Why do you do this to yourself, Bhoru?' He just smiled and shrugged it off.

One fine day, I wasn't so lucky. One of the seniors, 'Pathaan'—nicknamed by his coursemates after a certain 'special connection' he had with a girl from a different background—asked me one day, '*Oye*, have you seen my practical file?' I casually replied, 'Yes, sir. I saw your file in Kirmada's room.' He nodded and told me, 'Fine, get it back to me by evening.'

I nodded like it was a piece of cake, but when I went to Kirmada's room, no such file was to be found. I informed Pathaan about the missing file, thinking that would be the end of it. Big mistake.

He gave me five days to locate it, but I took my sweet time, doing absolutely nothing about it. Then came the deadline. That evening, Pathaan caught me in the anteroom just before dinner, his face like a thundercloud. He ordered me to search for it, dragging me across every room in the squadron. My study time went down the drain as I turned each room upside down, looking for that cursed file. But still, it was nowhere to be found.

By midnight, things escalated. Pathaan called for the entire Alpha Squadron, storming up to the Alpha Block's top floor. He lined us all up in the hallway, and his booming voice echoed through the building. 'You lot want to act clever, huh? No problem. Let's see how smart you feel after a little session.' He made us do rolls on the cold tiles, hands and legs burning as we moved like we were scrubbing the floor with our bodies.

The irony? As we huffed and puffed through the punishment, Pathaan's face lit up with a sudden realisation. After hours of searching and punishment, he checked his own room, and guess what? The file was right there, buried under a pile of his clothes.

We could barely hold back our groans. One of us whispered, 'Seriously, this guy made us all suffer for his own mess?' But, of course, he was the senior, so we were the ones to bear the brunt. And let's just say our 'loving' Alpha Squadron never let me forget that night.

In the end, while Pathaan couldn't actually punish us with anything, he came up with another brilliant idea. I was handed a hefty stack of Physics practical files to complete all the diagrams while Mushki got stuck with Chemistry. 'Consider it a bonding exercise,' Pathaan said with a grin. Yeah, bonding over the agony of completing practicals for seniors—just what I needed!

◆◆◆

The day our seniors got their much-deserved Liberty, the director, in all his wisdom, thought they were too 'exhausted' after their written exams. But we all knew the reality: it was our time to take over! As the seniors happily went off for their break, our Sunday suddenly became a playground for some... 'creative activities'.

Now, here's where it got interesting. One of our coursemates, who had a bit of a rebellious streak, smuggled in a 'boot'—our secret code for a mobile phone, a contraband item in the Academy. He had stashed it with his OD's blessing, and we all knew it was time for some entertainment. 'Pomeranian' had an idea. 'Boys, tonight we're hosting... a Moan Hub competition!' he announced with a straight face.

Now, I know, I know—sounds wild, right? But Pomeranian had already set the whole thing up. The venue? room number 36, where Alpha cadets and a few from Bravo and Charlie gathered. The event was unofficial, of course, but that didn't stop it from being the highlight of the week.

I, along with my fellow neighbour, Singla, was invited to join. But we both declined—I mean, as I've said before, I didn't even know the 'M' in Moan. But that refusal came with a catch: no participation, no audience seats. So, we were left listening from outside, like two confused spies, trying to decipher what was happening.

The judging panel was top-notch: Tatyaal, Gyani (the moaning maestro), and Pomeranian himself. The competition even had a title sponsor, 'Moan!'—with a logo that you can probably imagine yourself. Let's just say it involved a creative use of sound waves. The host for the night was 'Gaint', who kicked off the event with a dramatic flair, 'Welcome, gentlemen, to the most anticipated contest of the decade!'

As the participants stepped up, the room lit up with their 'performances'. Mushki gave it his all, sounding like he was trying to communicate with the underworld, while Khassi's effort resembled a goat stuck on a hill. 'Baghdadi' put up a solid performance, his deep baritone echoing through the walls, making the room sound like a haunted cave. 'Is that a moan, or are you starting a motorcycle, Baghdadi?' joked Gyani, sending everyone into fits of laughter. My buddy was next, and he surprised everyone with an unexpectedly smooth and melodic tone—no one saw that coming!

'Pujara', our cameraman, captured every moment (don't worry, this footage never left the room). After an hour of unrestrained hilarity, cheers, and attempts to muffle our laughs so we wouldn't get caught, the judges announced the winner: my buddy, GBR!

Gyani stood up, 'And the crown goes to... GBR! The guy who made us all doubt our own moaning skills!' Everyone roared in laughter, and Pomeranian, pretending to wipe a tear, added, 'Such talent. Truly a gift to mankind.'

My buddy was instantly a celebrity in our course for his 'unusual' talent. And as for me? Well, I suddenly realised that maybe it wouldn't hurt to have some of those... skills. You never know when a senior might call upon you for some weird tasks you were allotted with, right?

This night became legendary in our course's unofficial history, and even though it was all in fun, it gave us a much-needed break and a story to laugh about during those long, disciplined days. The videos still lie in our secret folders, making us laugh at what we used to do.

Boys and Blunders

Tam (time) se wapis aa jana!
—Warden Sahab

At last, right from the moment the clock struck, the much awaited time finally arrived—our first Liberty on October 2nd, 2022. Sure, it was Gandhi Jayanti for the rest of the country, but for us, it was our own personal Independence Day. We were practically floating in excitement, imagining all the things we could do outside the Academy gates. And how did we get it? Well, it took just a casual mention during a lecture in the PVH hall, and the director, to our absolute shock, agreed. It was like we'd found the cheat code to freedom.

Since it was our first Liberty, the warden was on high alert, his brows permanently furrowed with worry about how we'd handle the outside world. So, he cut the usual Liberty time down—9 a.m. to 4 p.m. instead of the usual 5 p.m. But did that dampen our spirits? Not a chance. The whole night before was buzzing with plans and whispers about 'muftis' and who was going where. The muftis were crisp, sharp, and, frankly, made us look like rockstars. We strutted around like we owned the town, and every shopkeeper and passerby turned their heads as if we were some celebrity squads.

◆◆◆

The morning of Liberty, everyone practically catapulted out of bed. Some skipped breakfast in the mess, eager to devour some 'real food' outside. Budgets varied wildly—some had 1000/-, others had just 500/-. But we were AFPIans, after all, so pooling resources was our speciality. With all of us contributing, everyone had enough to make it a day to remember.

When we hit the town, the chaos began. Pomeranian, always dramatic, spotted a hat shop and decided he needed a cowboy hat to complete his look. He haggled with the shopkeeper, saying, '*Bhaiya,* AFPI *wale hain,* discount *toh banta hai*!' The shopkeeper, clearly amused, couldn't resist and knocked down the price. Pomeranian wore that hat like he'd just won a pageant, tipping it to every girl who walked by. At one point, a girl actually rolled her eyes and muttered, '*Yeh* hero *ban raha hai kya*?' But that only made him tip the hat even more dramatically as if he was in some old-school Bollywood movie.

Meanwhile, Sariya and Balli found themselves in a game parlour, challenging each other to a round of shooting games. Sariya was hitting bullseyes like he was born for it, while Balli kept missing. After every shot, he'd scratch his head and say, '*Arre bhai,* wind *ka issue hai*!' Sariya smirked and said, '*Bhai, yeh* indoor game *hai, kahan se hawa aa rahi hai?'* Everyone burst out laughing as Balli tried to come up with more excuses, but Sariya just kept hitting those targets.

Then, there was Gyani, who, true to his name, found himself chatting up a bunch of kids at a park, giving them 'life lessons'. The kids looked puzzled, one of them asking, '*Bhaiya, yeh sach mein kaam karta hai?'* Gyani nodded with all the seriousness he could muster, '*Beta,* AFPI *ki baatein hain. Zindagi ke sab* lessons *yahin se milte hain.*' The kids just blinked at him, clearly more interested in their ice creams than his advice.

But the real chaos happened when Mushki and Baghdadi got caught in a bit of a scene outside a café. Mushki, being his usual clumsy self, was adjusting his Mufti, trying to get that perfect 'model-like' fold. Just as he was striking a pose, a group of girls walked by, one of them saying, '*Aise kya ban-ne ki koshish kar rahe ho?'* Mushki turned red, muttering under his breath, '*Arre yaar, ye* timing *bhi na!*' But the girls just laughed and walked away, leaving Mushki trying to look cool but failing miserably.

Meanwhile, Baghdadi—well, he had his own style. He'd somehow managed to convince the café guy that he was some big shot from an army family, flashing his mufti like it was his ticket to free snacks. At one point, a girl came up to him and said, '*Aap log* AFPI *se hain na? Bohot achhe lag rahe ho* uniform *mein.*' Baghdadi puffed out his chest, saying, '*Bas,* madam, duty *ka part hai,*' as if he was guarding the border himself. Gyani, standing nearby, couldn't resist adding, '*Haan haan,* border *ke bahar hi* duty *hai iski*—the café border!' The girl giggled, and Baghdadi shot Gyani a death glare, but even he couldn't hide his smile.

And then there was my own little moment that stayed with me. An elderly lady walked up to me, asking, '*Beta,* are you from AFPI?' I nodded, saying, 'Yes, ma'am. But how did you know?' She smiled and said, 'My son was an AFPIan too. Now he's a lieutenant.' That hit me like a ton of pride bricks. It was like a rush of realisation—being a part of something bigger, tied to a legacy that meant so much to so many people. As I looked around, seeing my coursemates acting like a bunch of overgrown kids in uniform, it felt like, just for a day, we were truly on top of the world.

And as the day came to an end, and we all gathered back at the Academy, there was a sense of accomplishment—not just in how much fun we had, but in the fact that we made our first Liberty count. Sure, we might have pushed a few boundaries, but it was all in good spirits. And there was a silent promise that next time, it'd be even better.

◆◆◆

After the high of our first Liberty, we barely had time to settle back into our routines before we got hit with the news of the next big event: Dussehra! It felt like the perfect chance to blow off steam again. And let me tell you, we had plans—plans that somehow miraculously came together.

The centrepiece of our celebration was our very own enactment of the Ram Leela. But being a boys-only Academy meant there was one glaring issue: we had no Sita. While we brainstormed, SP, our senior with a flair for drama, came up with the wildest idea. With a serious face, he declared, 'Tatyaal will be Sita!' The hall went silent for a second, then exploded into laughter. But Tatyaal didn't resist once he realised this was non-negotiable.

And so, Tatyaal was our Sita, with 'Sooden' cast as Ram. Bakra, with his springy energy, was naturally chosen as Ravan. As for the rest of us? We got the prestigious roles of the Vanar Sena and Rakshasa Sena. That's right—your boy here was one of the many monkeys in Hanuman's army. And the chaos that followed was pure gold comedy.

On the day of the grand performance, Guruji, with his purest Hindi, took on the role of the narrator, hyping up each scene like he was calling a cricket match. 'And here comes Ram to challenge Ravan!' he boomed. Sooden tried to puff out his chest, looking all heroic, while Tatyaal, decked in a makeshift saree made from bedsheets, tried his best to appear demure and... well, let's just say, the saree wasn't his thing.

Now came the final fight scene, and things got a little too real. Some of us in the Vanar sena got overexcited and decided to make a straight beeline for Ravana, aiming to take him down right then and there. From the sidelines, one of our seniors yelled, '*Oye*, you're the *Vanar Sena*, not Ram, boys! Get in character!' Immediately, we dropped to the ground, scratching our heads like confused monkeys, mumbling, 'Yes, sir, we're back in character.'

The 'battle' was a mess, with the sena members falling over each other, some carefully positioning themselves so they wouldn't dirty their freshly washed uniforms from the laundry. One of the guys even tried folding his legs like a yogi mid-fight, all to save his pants from the Academy's notorious mud patches. Meanwhile, Tatyaal, playing his role as Sita, gave Sooden a look that said, 'Hurry up and finish this before I trip over this saree.'

Finally, when Bakra—our valiant Ravana—collapsed dramatically to the ground, it was time to burn the effigy. The Ravana effigy itself was a masterpiece of cardboard boxes, hastily decorated with markers and stuffed with local firecrackers courtesy of some well-connected local cadets. As the flames caught, we all cheered until the first firecracker misfired and zoomed straight towards the mess contractor, who was standing nearby, looking rather unimpressed.

It was as if even the Ravana effigy was on our side, rebelling against the same bland breakfast we'd had that morning. 'Maybe he's mad about that watery milk, too!' someone shouted, and the whole sena cracked up.

This Dussehra celebration was something else—chaotic, hilarious, and the kind of memory that sticks with you. It turned out to be one of those days where, for a moment, you felt like nothing could go wrong... even when it very clearly did.

◆◆◆

October was anything but fun for us, especially with Kirmada's birthday just around the corner. We had planned the ultimate surprise, ready to unleash our collective trickery upon him. The first step? Lock him in a room right after the fall-in, leaving him with no escape from our birthday antics. But little did we know that the night would take a turn for the ridiculous, thanks to the guard on duty, affectionately nicknamed 'Kauwa'. If anyone was going to keep an eye on us, it was definitely this guy—like a hawk, or rather, a very grumpy crow.

As we prepared for Kirmada's big night, chaos unfolded when one of our fellow cadets, in a moment of pure panic, got himself into a pickle. When Kauwa demanded to know his name, our man blurted out, 'Room number 1, sir! My name is Teji!' Now, to clarify, 'Teji' was actually our bus driver—sitting back at home, blissfully unaware of the chaos unfolding in the Academy. But thanks to the guard's ignorance, he took this declaration at face value and nodded sagely.

The next day, during school fall-in, the warden strode into the courtyard, eyes scanning the ranks of cadets like a hawk on the hunt. Suddenly, he stopped dead in his tracks, pointing dramatically at a pair of slippers lying haphazardly near the guard post. 'Who owns these slippers?' he boomed, his voice echoing across the parade ground.

Silence fell over the assembly like a heavy fog. No one dared to claim them. I half-expected a dramatic courtroom scene, complete with finger-pointing and accusations, but instead, we were met with utter crickets. I wouldn't be surprised if those slippers ended up in the Academy museum—an eternal testament to our night of shenanigans.

But the real kicker was yet to come. After the slipper debacle, the warden announced he would be doing a uniform check. My stomach dropped. I hadn't shaved! As he strode towards me, I was convinced I'd be dragged in front of the director alongside my buddies who were recently caught by the interviewing officer for wandering outside their cabins during study periods. 'Great,' I thought, 'I'll be sharing their punishment today. Just what I wanted.'

As the warden pointed at me, his expression as serious as a drill sergeant, I braced myself for the worst. 'Report to me after school,' he declared. My heart raced at the thought of facing the director, and my mind conjured up images of what kind of punishment awaited me. 'Maybe they'll just get a slap on the wrist,' I mused. 'Or maybe they'll have to scrub the toilets with toothbrushes! Wouldn't that be a laugh?'

When I finally escaped from school and hurried to the warden's office, I half expected to see my friends already sweating it out in their chairs, awaiting their fates. But as I arrived, I learned that the warden had completely forgotten about my beard situation! I could hardly believe my luck.

As I walked out, I caught a glimpse of my buddies, who had just received their punishment. 'Seven ETs!' one of them groaned, and I couldn't help but chuckle. 'At least you guys have each other for moral support,' I teased. 'Or maybe I should say, you've got seven extra hours of quality time together!'

'Very funny,' one replied, 'but just wait until we get you next time!'

'Yeah, yeah,' I said with a smirk. 'But for now, I'm just glad to be clean-shaven and free!'

◆◆◆

As winter approached, the director thought it'd be the perfect time to kick us into high gear with the 'Higher Test'. Apparently, the chill in the air wasn't enough motivation, so we were in for some 'extra heat'. Rajinder Sahab stood at the starting line, his voice booming like a drill sergeant on a megaphone, reminding us, 'Twelve minutes! No exceptions!'

The moment the timer started, we took off like our lives depended on it. But within the first 500 m, it became clear that half of us were sprinting while the other half looked like we were jogging to the nearest chai stall. Somehow, though, everyone managed to cross the finish line in time, huffing and puffing like a herd of wounded animals. As one guy wheezed, '*Yaar*, I'm ready for a medal,' another snorted and replied, 'Yeah, for best dramatic performance on a three-kilometre run!'

Then came the challenge for the poor souls who hadn't passed the BPT (Basic Physical Test) last time. They had to earn their redemption by doing push-ups. I was part of this unfortunate squad, bracing myself. As I was struggling through my last few push-ups, Rajinder Sahab gave me a knowing smirk and shouted, 'Sharma *ji, lagta hai aapka dil bahut bada hai*—four more, for the girlfriend you don't have yet!'

The laughter was contagious. My instructor cracked a joke at my expense, and my buddies, trying not to burst out in front of him, muttered their own comebacks in the softest whispers and said, '*Bhai, ek push-up uske liye bhi, jo abhi tak tujhe* notice *bhi nahi karti!*' I couldn't help but laugh, and somehow, I cranked out those last few push-ups, fuelled by the teasing.

Just when we thought we'd finally get a break, Rajinder Sahab decided to up the ante. 'Rope climbing next! Line up!' My stomach dropped as I eyed the ropes hanging ominously, but I remembered a few tricks that Atma Sahab had taught us. As I was hauling myself up, gritting my teeth, I overheard someone below whisper, '*Yaar,* Sharma *ji, ek aur* push-up *uske liye jo tera naam bhi nahi jaanti!*' I nearly lost my grip, laughing.

After rope climbing, we faced the toe-touch challenge. A few guys raised their hands right away, admitting defeat. The director's face grew darker with every hand that shot up, and then—almost like a broken record—more hands went up for the chin-up test. That was it. The director lost his patience. 'It's the end of the year, and half of you can't do toe-touches or chin-ups?' He turned to the PTI and muttered, 'Make sure they feel this in their bones. Increase PT intensity from now on.'

From that day onward, 100 push-ups became our daily 'warm-up'. It didn't matter if you did them properly or looked like a lopsided snake trying to slither uphill. Some of us could barely feel our arms by push-up sixty, yet the count never stopped. And then came the worst part: Rajinder Sahab's 'quality checks'. He'd stop and 'inspect' every wrong push-up, giving us a look that said, 'Just you wait.' Then he'd yell, 'Reset count!' as we groaned. We couldn't dare protest because, as experience had taught us, he'd just smirk and add five more to the count.

On especially tough days, we'd joke with each other between breaths. '*Bhai, ek aur uske liye jo teri* good morning *ka* reply *bhi nahi deti!*' If someone was struggling through a round, his friend would say, '*Arrey yaar, char aur laga na! Soch us ladki ke baare mein jo keh rahi thi "tumhe dekha toh kuch kuch hota hai!"*' There was always laughter mixed with our groans, making the brutal workouts a little lighter.

Eventually, the seniors got roped into our suffering, too, since they couldn't escape the PT regimen. Some of them would look at us with a mix of pity and amusement, especially after Rajinder Sahab's infamous 'let's start over' announcements. And the cycle continued day after day.

Finally, during a particularly brutal set of chin-ups, one of my buddies whispered, '*Bas bhai, ab toh koi bhi* girlfriend *mil jaaye toh main uske liye 500* push-ups *laga dunga!*' We all burst out laughing mid-chin-up, which only got us another set of five. By the end of it, we couldn't feel our arms, but we had at least managed to keep our spirits high (or as high as they could be with the director and PTI breathing down our necks).

Every painful rep was like our own little tribute, each push-up dedicated to an imaginary girlfriend who might have been unimpressed anyway. And just because of my PTI's unique 'motivational techniques', each one of my coursemates was ready to hype each other for a girl we didn't know—a girl who, undoubtedly, didn't know us either!

The Diwali Dilemma

Aap sabko Diwali ki Happy Diwali!
—PTI Rajinder Sahab

Rushes of excitement surged through every cadet the second we heard the words 'Diwali Break'. It was like an electric wave that ran through the entire Academy. This was the second time we were heading home, and if there was any ounce of formality left in us, it was swept away by the thought of home-cooked meals, family celebrations, and a good five days away from these walls. As soon as we got the green light, everyone was already mentally packing their bags, their minds drifting back to familiar faces and festive lights.

As we filed back through the Academy gates, there was a kind of chaotic energy that only a pack of teens returning from a five-day break could bring. Bags in hand, we were all lined up for the guard's inspection, and the stakes were high—especially for those who'd taken the risk of sneaking in some 'contraband'. Of course, there were whispered rumours about the infamous 'boots' making a comeback, our classic code word for mobile phones. Everyone's nerves were on edge, yet the smirks and half-suppressed laughs betrayed how much we missed this madness.

'Open your bag,' the guard muttered, not even bothering to look us in the eyes as he dug into one bag after another. We'd catch each other's eyes, silently daring one another not to crack. As one guy's stash of sweets tumbled out, everyone within earshot burst into laughter.

'Bro, trying to open a candy shop in here?' someone quipped as the guard held up the treats.

'Oh, just wait until they find the real stash tonight,' another whispered, eyes darting with mischief as everyone nodded. We knew a raid was coming—it was practically a tradition on our return, a grand unveiling of every secret snack and cleverly hidden 'boot'.

But as they searched through our bags, we were all quietly thinking the same thing: for all the sweets, socks, and '*boots*' we might have hidden, what we were really bringing back was a bit of the warmth we'd felt back home. And now, as we stood together, side-by-side, facing the scrutiny of the guards and laughing at each other's ridiculousness, it felt like we'd brought a new piece of family back here, too.

But here's the thing we didn't expect. After just five days, stepping back through those Academy gates felt like coming home all over again. The hugs, the teasing, and the laughter that greeted us—it all felt like we'd been away for ages. And that's when it hit us. Somehow, this Academy, these people, they'd become just as much family as those waiting for us at home. The Academy had turned into our new home—a home away from home.

As the guards continued their inspections, we began sizing each other up, realising how different everyone looked after just five days. Some had clearly indulged a bit too much at home, while others looked like they'd hardly slept, maybe thanks to late-night Diwali festivities. With each bag that passed inspection, our teasing ramped up—because what's a reunion without a little friendly fire? Just as one of the guys heaved his overstuffed bag past the guards, someone in the crowd couldn't resist:

Someone from the back yelled, 'Sharma *ji! Tum toh ghar pe jaate hi apna* bag pack *kar rahe honge, bas yahan wapas aane ke liye!*'

Laughter echoed through the hall; each laugh layered with relief, warmth, and a feeling of belonging that no holiday could replace. We didn't just belong to an Academy; we belonged to each other. As we unpacked our bags and settled back into the daily rhythm, the truth was clear: the real family, the one that made every day a celebration, was right here, within these walls.

◆◆◆

As the clouds fell dark and the halls grew silent, the night raid squad got ready for action. Bags were lined up like trophies, ready to be gutted for hidden treasures. The more they collected, the better the feast ahead. Some guys, knowing resistance was futile, surrendered their stashes immediately. Others tried to act innocent as if they'd only packed books and fresh uniforms.

That's when our secret weapon, 'Chuha', came into play. His nickname wasn't for nothing; the guy could open a locked bag in under ten seconds, no tools required. With a mischievous grin, he cracked open each bag like a safecracker on a mission. And the haul was incredible—seriously, a treasure trove. From premium biscuits to luxury chocolates, juice boxes, and, of course, the golden prize: instant noodles.

'*Arrey bhai*, who brought the Swiss chocolates? Whose family is this loaded?' someone joked, holding up a shiny box.

'Swiss chocolate? *Bhai*, I thought I packed those for my sister!' came a defensive reply, but the chocolate stayed in the communal pile.

Then came the noodles piled up like we were prepping for a winter famine. '*Bas ab yahi bacha tha,* Maggi *ka* stock *ho gaya!*' someone laughed, eyeing the stacks of instant noodles. And sure enough, we had a plan. Not that a hot kettle was exactly regulation, but somehow, someone had managed to smuggle one in. You'd think we were running a five-star noodle joint the way guys were lining up.

And here's the truth: kettle Maggi? Better than anything from a stove. Maybe it was the thrill of breaking a rule or just the joy of doing it together, but man, it tasted like heaven.

The stash we collected was enormous. It could've fed an army—or at least an entire hostel for a few nights. All the goodies were piled high in the sergeant's room. Biscuits, sweets, chocolates—distributed equally, of course. Well, almost.

'First come, first served,' yelled one of the guys as he grabbed an oversized chocolate bar, earning a wave of groans and laughter from the rest.

'*Arrey, mere wale se kahan gaya?*' a guy exclaimed, his hands rummaging through the remaining snacks, while another shot back, '*Bhai, jo haath lag gaya woh uska!*'

As for those 'sneaky' cadets with secret hiding spots, well, we all knew about those too. '*Koi baat nahi, bhai.* Share *kar lena jab zaroorat ho,*' someone teased, shooting a look at one guy in the corner, clearly guarding his backpack like it contained state secrets.

And so, in true AFPI fashion, the snacks disappeared faster than anyone anticipated. By the end of the week, we were back to mess food, sharing stories of that legendary stash raid that lived on in Academy lore. And every now and then, someone would joke, '*Arrey, kabhi kabhi sochta hoon ke bas ek* kettle *aur* Maggi *rahe, aur kuch nahi chahiye.*'

◆◆◆

As we'd barely settled back in from Diwali break, the discipline we'd held onto so tight at home seemed to unravel at the Academy. It was like a test—to see how long we could keep up the behaviour our families loved to see, though we all knew that wouldn't last. By lunchtime, it was already showing; the entire dining hall was buzzing. No officials were around that day due to some work, and we took advantage of it, talking at full volume. But just when we thought we were safe, one senior strode in and cut through the chatter with a single order, 'Silence.'

We clammed up instantly, but it was short-lived. At dinner, the same thing happened. We thought we'd try our luck again, and naturally, the same senior reappeared, but this time he was not letting it slide. After a long moment of watching us ignore his orders, his face hardened, and he barked. As the senior laid down his orders, it was clear he was not taking any chances. 'Alpha, Bravo, Charlie—you'll fall in at the top floor of "A" block,' he announced, 'and let me make this clear. Alpha reports at 9:30 a.m. sharp, Bravo at 10 a.m., and Charlie at 10:30 a.m.' His voice was steely, making sure each squadron knew the time slots down to the last minute. The message was clear: he'd set the schedule to keep us apart, but we all understood this was more than just timing—it was his way of making sure each group got their own personal 'lesson' without interference.

In their rooms, before heading to the spot, each squadron had a moment to exchange glances and whispers.

In Alpha, Dada muttered, 'Guess we're getting our Diwali "gifts" this year.'

Lahsun shrugged, 'Nothing we didn't expect. But hey, at least we're first and can get it over with.'

In Bravo, Balli laughed, 'Look on the bright side, guys—by the time we're up, they might be too tired to make us do much.'

Macchi rolled his eyes, 'Yeah, keep dreaming, Balli. I'm sure they're saving the best for us.'

Meanwhile, in Charlie, Marcos stretched his legs, trying to prepare. 'Alright, boys, we know the drill. Just keep your heads down; no funny business.'

Bhoru grinned, 'Yeah, Marcos, I'll just stay silent as a statue. You believe that?'

Malhi snickered, 'As long as you keep your jokes in your head, Bhoru, we might survive.'

Each squadron went up at its designated time. When Alpha reported at 9:30 a.m., they lined up silently, their faces serious. The senior didn't waste time.

'Alpha! Start frog jumps, now!' he barked. The squad began, the thuds of their boots filling the hallway.

Sooden shot a quick look at Dada but kept going, silently enduring. Once Alpha's session ended, they exchanged weary looks as they were dismissed, their silence speaking volumes.

Next came Bravo at 10 a.m. The senior gave them similar instructions, and the whole squad began their exercises. Balli gritted his teeth, murmuring to Sariya just loud enough for him to hear, 'Remind me never to cheer for freedom again.'

Sariya barely managed a tired grin. 'Noted.'

Finally, the Charlie Squadron filed in at 10:30 a.m., and by then, the senior seemed even more irritated. They lined up, keeping straight faces, ready for whatever was to come.

'Charlie! You boys seemed extra lively today,' the senior said with a raised brow. 'Think you're tough, do you? Let's see you survive squats till I say stop!'

Moan couldn't resist a quick look at Marcos as they began, who gave him a silent nod as if to say, keep quiet, keep going.

But after inspecting each squadron, the senior was clearly unsatisfied. So, he made the rounds again, declaring that we'd be falling in the next night, this time with Charlie reporting first.

Now, you should know that something strange mostly happened when Charlie was about to face a punishment. Somehow, our warden would show up out of nowhere—twice, it had happened with Charlie already—and tonight was no exception. The minute Charlie started doing frog jumps, their shoes echoing on the floor with each jump, we all knew.

From my room, I heard the familiar click of the warden's footsteps on the floor. The warden marched in, demanding an explanation, and the senior began, saying it was due to 'discipline issues'. Just then, there was a knock at my door, and I opened it to see the warden himself, asking for a paper and pen to record names.

Then, as if on cue, the Interviewing Officer (IO) himself appeared. His expression was hard as he demanded to know why the punishment was taking place. I'd never seen him act this way before. What it ended with was the senior was immediately suspended for a month.

It wasn't that punishments were banned; no, this was an unspoken pact. Seniors could discipline us and keep the incident from going higher up, knowing that if the director heard about it, expulsion would be inevitable. Every visitor, whether a lieutenant or a captain, always reminded us, 'Respect your seniors. Their orders are your fate.' It was a simple truth: if you messed up, you had to answer for it. And deep down, we understood that these trials were part of what we'd signed up for—the path we had to walk to become the best of the best.

◆◆◆

By now, the winter had settled in, and we Titans were always warm, not just with our coats but with a '*jung* blood (the warden's heavily accented version of "young blood")' that ran hotter than ever. As the warden once put it, '*Jung* blood isn't just energy; it's the fire that young men carry when they're ready to serve, the drive that doesn't cool down even in the hardest winters.' It was a hard, powerful truth he'd impressed on us, and we could feel it with each step forward, knowing that this spirit was ours to carry. Being fresh cadets, our pride in AFPI ran deep, and our loyalty to each other was as strong as steel. Life at the Academy was a mix of rigorous training and light-hearted moments that bonded us in unexpected ways.

One afternoon, during the school break, Balli was on his way to the school shop for a little birthday celebration for one of our guys. AFPI birthday parties were a whole scene—everybody chipped in a bit, and Tatyaal, our unofficial 'finance minister', would handle the money like he was running a major operation. The birthday boy himself would stand beside him, dutifully passing out everything from lassi to patties, brownies, and, of course, chips and kurkure for the crowd still lingering around, trying to know if someone had extra snacks.

As Balli neared the shop, an overenthusiastic cadet from another Academy, 'Lattu', decided to pull a quick one. Just as Balli was passing, Lattu slid his leg out and tripped him. Down went Balli, barely missing from falling on the ground. It was like time froze. For us Titans, a fall was maybe nothing but disrespecting the uniform. That was war.

A murmur went through our crowd as a few of the boys—Mushki, Gyani, and Bakra—stepped up without hesitation, leaving their brownies behind and marching straight towards Lattu and his gang. Voices were raised, but before things could get too heated, the teachers swooped in like hawks, breaking it up before any 'lessons' were taught. Meanwhile, about eight of us were stuck back in class, practically clawing at the walls, not allowed to come out and join in the 'festivities'.

Soon, a bus arrived, summoned by the principal himself, and the guys who had confronted Lattu and company were sent straight back to the Academy. And there we were—the unfortunate eight left in the classroom, looking at each other, knowing we'd be carrying not just books but the bags of everyone who had just left in a blaze of glory.

When we got back to the Academy, sure enough, the entire crew was waiting, ready to remind us just how we'd 'left them in the dust' while they went to defend Balli's honour. They didn't want to hear excuses at first; they only saw us as 'classroom deserters'. But after a few good laughs, they let us back into the circle, especially once they saw us lugging in about five bags each, looking like exhausted porters at the end of a long shift.

A few days later, the IO called in the boys who had confronted Lattu. He praised their loyalty, saying, 'You showed what it means to be a true cadet. But remember, this isn't a battleground just yet. Next time, let the seniors handle it.' We nodded, holding back grins, knowing that if it came to protecting our own dignity, the Titans wouldn't hesitate for a second.

In the end, though, we learned something that day: in AFPI, it wasn't just about discipline, training, or even the code of conduct. It was about a bond that ran deep, a loyalty that couldn't be shaken. And on those chilly winter mornings, when our blood was boiling and bonds were tested, we knew that no matter what, we'd stand by each other—ready to carry on each other's bags, lassi, or even grudges if needed.

Races, Ragda, and Rolling

Go ho gya! Gate ko touch and back, pehle das rakhunga
—DI Swaran Sahab

Even weeks before the sports meet at our school, the air was thick with anticipation. It was like the Diwali of all events, sparking excitement that spread across every corner. But for us AFPIans, it wasn't just about participation; it was a full-on mission to dominate and collect trophies like they were Pokémon. It was the time to prove the AFPIan blood again and show the so-called private defence academies why they are not AFPIans. The event took place on the sprawling grounds of a prestigious government university in the city, with towering guards stationed like mini-mountains, ready to halt any hint of mischief. The bouncer's loyal cronies hovered around, acting as if they could actually keep us in check.

But who were they kidding? AFPIans are a breed apart. Under the sharp eyes of those guards, we found ways to slip past unnoticed, using stealth techniques that would make ninjas jealous. Amidst all the rules and restrictions, there was always one name whispered with an amused grin whenever someone sneaked away for a break:

DST, fondly known as Doctor Sahab. DST wasn't just known for his stellar academics; he was revered (and teased) for his unending love of tea. The man was so obsessed with chai that it seemed to fuel his legendary intellect. Jokes flew that his PhD was in 'Advanced Chai Studies'.

During the sports meet, between the sprints and throws, DST's chai antics continued at full throttle. Every few minutes, there he was, weaving through the crowd with the agility of a pro athlete to secure another cup. We'd nudge each other and whisper, 'Doctor Sahab *ki chai* break *phir shuru ho gayi. Bhai, iska* viva *bhi chai pe hi hoga.*'

But when chai wasn't available, DST had a backup plan: coffee. If he was spotted near the stall with a cup of coffee, someone would mutter, '*Lagta hai chai ki dukaan band ho gayi aaj.*' Doda would add, 'Doctor Sahab *ne* coffee *pe* switch *kiya matlab* emergency *lagi hai.*' DST, hearing this, would give a dramatic nod and say, '*Bhai,* research *ka sawal hai, chai ho ya* coffee, mission complete *karna padta hai.*'

Even in the Academy, though tea was forbidden, Dr DST always had a way to keep his caffeine cravings under control. He'd stock up on instant coffee pouches in his room and mix them with milk from the mess to create his own brew. On days when he craved tea, he'd pull out tea pouches and, with milk stealthily borrowed from the ever-resourceful Tehla's Mall, brew the tea in an electric kettle, transforming his room into an undercover café. His addiction to caffeine was so strong that even the director somehow knew about it, and my coursemate, NSG, went to lengths to hide his specially imported coffee, only for him to find some other source.

◆◆◆

Our mornings started before the sun even clocked in. We would storm the field before any other school student dared to arrive. Seniors strutted in, their swagger so intense it could rival a Bollywood hero's entry. The seniors, with their serious faces, looked like they were ready to pose for the cover of *GQ*, though their actual talent was in making us laugh. We, the juniors, held back giggles, trying not to earn an early morning PT session for 'laughing without cause'. Because, let's face it, a senior's 'serious' look could make even a statue crack a smile!

The sports events were an absolute circus—we AFPIans, the ringmasters! Imagine all four competitors from each house being AFPIans. It's like being asked to choose between chocolate and more chocolate. Who do you even support? You'd look left, then right, and then just give up and shout, 'AFPI! AFPI!' like a confused but very enthusiastic sheep trying to find the herd. In the end, it didn't matter who got the first, second, or third position—because we knew AFPI was taking the gold. Always.

And then came the moment: AFPI versus another Academy. Now, this was the real deal. Forget the house. Forget your housemates. The only thing that mattered was whether our chant could shatter eardrums. I remember one of my senior AFPIans, who was also the house captain of another house, looked at the scoreboard and then at the crowd and said, 'Forget my house, let's just chant AFPI so loud that even the opposition gets scared.' And that's exactly what we did—suddenly, it was no longer about house pride. It was about the AFPI pride. Forget sportsmanship; we were going for AFPIan-ship.

And there was this one moment when someone from another Academy, who didn't know the sacred AFPI chant, dared to say, 'But your house isn't even winning, you know?' Without missing a beat, one of our AFPI brothers turned to him and said, 'Yeah, you're right, we're not winning... but we're about to dominate your ears with AFPI, so buckle up!' And we did. The stadium shook, the ground trembled, and I'm pretty sure the other Academy's morale evaporated faster than water on a hot pan.

In every game, no matter what the event was and no matter who was competing, AFPI was the true winner. It didn't matter if we were losing—we were winning the only thing that counted: volume. 'Who's going to win the game?' someone asked. And we all screamed in unison, 'It's AFPI! Always has been. Always will be!'

Honestly, who needs to win medals when you've already won the AFPI domination trophy in every competition?

But of course, this mostly prideful competition has its own moments of chaos featuring us, the juniors, many of us having taken part just for fun and to fill in the empty slots.

The long jump was first, and Moan, whose confidence was taller than him, prepared himself. Bhoru yelled, 'Moan, *piche dekho piche, gadda hai.* Jump *nahi,* parkour *karna padega kya?'* Moan rolled his eyes so hard they almost didn't return. He launched into the jump, landing midway and earning NSG's classic clap and commentary, '*Bhai,* Olympian *ki tarah gaya, nukkad ke* player *jaise gira.*' Even the judges struggled to suppress their laughter.

The shot-put event featured our very own gentle giant, Gaint. As he took the position, Marcos whispered to Malhi, '*Arre,* shot put *nahi,* Earth *ka* rotation *rukwane aya hai.*' Gaint hurled the shot put with the power of a Bollywood hero's punch, narrowly missing the guard's foot. The guard jumped back, glaring with eyes that screamed '*bachke rehna re baba.*' Bhoru quipped, 'Guard Sahab, warm-up *tha. Agla* throw stadium *ke bahar jayega.*' The guard's lips twitched in an almost-smile.

Next was the relay race, a spectacle of chaos. Kirmada and Malhi's baton exchange resembled a wrestling match more than a hand-off. Baba, waiting at the next leg, bounced as if his shorts were on fire. Seniors, more excited than us, shouted, '*Lage raho,* juniors, sports *nahi,* comedy show *lag raha hai!*'

The true magic of the meet wasn't just in the events; it was in how our seniors became legends. At the end of the day, they'd slap us on the back and say, '*Aaj raat ka* treat *hamare* side *se,* but *koi pakda gaya toh* ET *khud ki hai!*' This was met with whoops and cheers as they handed out pizzas and drinks. We'd laugh till we had stitches, bonding over stories and playful taunts.

The bus ride back to the Academy was pure cinema. Seniors had a ritual—hooking up their *boots* to speakers and blasting music so loud it could wake the dead. Desi beats thumped through the bus while the driver, half-smirking, mouthed along, pretending not to notice our aisle-turned-dance floor.

This short journey back to the Academy also became the hub for sharing legendary stories, one of them being Mister Funky Feet's epic fail. One senior cackled, '*Usne* socks bucket *mein daale,* wash *ke liye, bhool gaya poora mahina!*' Another jumped in, '*Bhai, itni khatarnaak smell thi,* floor *pe* map *ki zaroorat nahi thi. Naak* follow *karo,* epicentre *mil jayega!*' The socks had become so notorious that when Funky Feet remembered them, they had to be discarded like a secret CIA operation. He buried them in the Academy's waste pit, muttering, '*Koi na, yeh bhi ek* mission *hai.*'

But here's the thing: Funky Feet wasn't even his real name. It was a temporary one, a nickname thrown around by our seniors for the story, as they never wanted to use his real name in front of the juniors, not out of disrespect but because it was all about course loyalty. In the Academy, no matter how much trouble you got into, the coursemates had each other's backs, especially when it came to keeping each other's dignity intact in front of the juniors. So, Funky Feet it was—and the true identity of the 'socks assassin' stayed a well-kept secret among the seniors.

Now, who could forget Operation Samosa Suraksha—a full-blown mission, with the school setting up a stall for all the students to get their hands on *samosas*, *burfi*, juice, and bananas? But let's be real, one round was never enough for us. We went for rounds two, three, and sometimes, if we were feeling bold, even a fourth. Every time we snuck up to the stall, we'd try our best to act innocent, as if we weren't plotting to sneak a second (or third) round. But sometimes, the staff would catch on. That's when we'd go into full-on 'crisis mode'. One of us would whisper, 'Sir, *bhookh lag rahi hai,*' with the most convincing, wide-eyed expression we could muster, hoping it would work. And it usually did.

The real fun began when our teacher—bless her heart—caught onto the operation and decided to join in. She marched up to the staff with a serious face and said, 'Some of them didn't get their share.' Next thing you know, we were back at the stall, piling up our plates with *samosas* like we were preparing for a famine. Of course, we tried to play it cool, but we all knew the game was on. We couldn't have enough samosas, *burfi*, and juice, and we were getting away with it, one round at a time.

By the end of the sports meet, we were on cloud nine. Though there was just one 'Best Athlete' award to be given out, we bagged two, for two of our seniors performed the best equally throughout the meet, and we weren't about to let that moment pass without celebration. With at least sixty medals under our belt, including twenty-five golds, we had truly dominated the competition.

To celebrate our victories, we jumped straight into a round of push-ups. 'One, AFPI! Two, AFPI! Three, AFPI!' we shouted, counting our way all the way to twenty, with every descent into the push-up followed by a loud, unified 'AFPI!' as we came back up. The energy was through the roof, and we could feel the ground shaking with the force of our *josh*. All the other students, both from the academies as well as the Shemrockites, the seniors as well as juniors, watched in awe as we completed our celebration.

Once the push-ups were done, there was no stopping us. We gathered together and let out our war cry—louder and stronger than ever before: '*Nischay Kar Apni Jeet Karoon!*' We had absolutely ruled the ground, and it felt like nothing could stand in our way.

As the celebrations continued, I looked around at the medals and trophies in the hands of my coursemates. I didn't have a single one myself, but I felt a sense of pride and respect that no trophy could match. Being an AFPIan wasn't about the awards—it was about the unity, the strength, and the bond we shared. This meet may have been an inter-house event, but we AFPIans were one throughout it. I could feel it in every moment, in every shout, in every push-up. We weren't just a group of cadets—we were a family. The coursemates around me weren't just friends or teammates—they were brothers. Maybe not by blood, but by soul, we were united as one. That's the spirit of AFPI—strong, proud, and unbreakable FAMILY.

◆◆◆

After the grand sports meet, the atmosphere was different. The seniors, usually distant and stern, seemed almost approachable. Maybe it was the shared victories or the collective pride, but there was a newfound ease between them and us. Of course, the discipline and respect remained; there was no crossing that line.

One night, around 11 o'clock, we were lounging in our rooms, replaying the highlights of the past few days. That's when I noticed that Malhi, the quiet genius known for going to bed at nine sharp, was still wide awake. His eyes had a glint that only meant one thing: mischief. Tatyaal, the usual instigator, exchanged a grin with Sooden and Dada, and within minutes, the team was assembled—Malhi, Tatyaal, Sooden, Gaint, and Dada. The plan was simple: create chaos.

They snuck up to the seniors' corridor, knocked on a door, and sprinted to the next room before the senior even opened it. Confused, the senior stepped out, rubbing his eyes and muttering, probably assuming his own friends were at it again. But then came the masterstroke: the boys locked the door from the outside and banged on it hard before melting back into the shadows. The senior called out to a friend, only to realise that none of them were responsible. The cold winter night only added to the confusion.

I was soundly asleep in my room when, at 11:45 p.m., my buddy, GBR, burst into my room, out of breath. 'Get up! Seniors *ne* ground floor *pe bulaya hai*!'

Within five minutes, the whole course was lined up in the chill, shivering from nerves and cold. It was chaos. The seniors paced in front of us, trying to count heads while we shifted restlessly. Kumbhkaran, true to his name, started dozing off while standing. I nudged him with my elbow. '*Yahan mat so, warna gir jaayega*!'

'Who did this?' one senior asked sharply. We looked around, some genuinely confused about what had happened, others playing along. Nobody stepped forward. Anda, who'd just undergone a DNS (Deviated Nasal Septum) surgery, got called out. 'Anda, you look too relaxed. Here's your task,' a senior said, tossing him a stack of newspapers. 'Underline every "N, D, A" you find. Prove your dedication to your goal. And yes, don't forget to count the letters thereafter.'

The rest of us held back laughter. Anda's face was a mix of disbelief and silent resignation as he sat down to work. The seniors barked, 'Push-up position!' and we dropped instantly. This wasn't one of those moments where we'd shout 'AFPI' with pride; it was sheer discipline. We counted internally, focusing on each move.

The night's tension rose after the push-ups, and before we could catch our breath, a senior barked, 'Rolling position! From the end stairs to the water cooler and back—don't stop!'

We exchanged silent glances. The rolling punishment was infamous; it wasn't just exhausting; it was a chaotic symphony of groans and whispers. As we began to roll, one by one, the world spun around us, the cold biting at our ears. The ice-cold floor was freezing our backs.

Rolling back and forth, the cooler loomed like an unreachable oasis. The seniors looked on, arms crossed, hiding smirks behind their stern faces.

'Frog jumps, line up!' The command made us groan internally. We lined up, thighs burning, and hopped like frogs, the cold air now mixed with the heat radiating from our muscles.

'Kumbhkaran, *ab tu so nahi raha?*' I whispered, smirking. He half-smiled, '*Bhai, yeh sapna hi lag raha hai, bas* end *nahi ho raha.*'

'Handstands!' The final challenge came, and we staggered into position. Cold sweat dripped, and noses brushed the floor. Despite the strain, not a single soul broke formation.

Winters had never felt this heated, but we pushed through, each punishment a badge of our collective stubbornness. We might have been reprimanded, but no senior or warden could break the unspoken bond we had as a course. That night, laughter was swallowed, jokes shared through side glances, and unity tested.

We ended up exhausted, sprawled like fallen soldiers on the ground, but still, no one spoke a name. With a last warning of '2 a.m. again, if names don't come out,' the seniors finally retreated. Silence blanketed us, but beneath it was a pulse of shared triumph.

Malhi whispered just loud enough for those near him to hear, '*Inko bhi* fun *chahiye lagta hai.*' We smirked, careful not to get caught. No one spoke up. We knew the drill: unity over everything.

Eventually, Malhi and the others stepped forward, owning up to their prank. The rest of us were relieved and impressed—it took guts. Their 'reward' was a luxurious Sunday filled with everything no one ever wanted at AFPI, but no one regretted it. We left that night tired but united. The bond we shared wasn't just course mate camaraderie; it was brotherhood, not by blood but by shared soul.

The Winter of Chaos

Aaj garam paani aa rha tha!?
Noooo, sirrrr.

Moments before the year-end arrived, everything had wrapped up—all the games and competitions were done, leaving behind memories filled with the best of *josh*. During these events, rivalry between the squadrons was fierce. But honestly, who could break the brotherhood that we had? Any tension never lasted more than three days—the typical length of a competition. This time, though, there was a shift in the air. For the first time, the Alpha Squadron was leading in everything, and now it was time for the most important competition: cross country. This was when all our boys would run their hearts out for 5 km, break records, and earn glory. The whole Academy was buzzing with energy.

The cross-country event was legendary not just because it decided the banner winner but also because it signalled the official end of PT. Trust me, that news made us happier than getting a surprise Sunday movie screening in PVH.

Every competition had its own unique touch, and the best part was how we motivated our own squadron while making the others feel like they were on the losing side. And it was all fair game! We invented chants and slogans for each occasion. The Bravo Squadron, known for winning the trophy each year, was often greeted with, '*Ikki dukki khen ni deni,* Bravo *nu* trophy *len ni deni*!' The Apaches and Cheetahs had united throughout the year for one sole mission: to break the ego of the Braves and make a new legacy.

We'd also raise eyebrows in the opponent's direction, chanting, 'Blackout! Blackout!' to psych them out. The air was always charged with the continuous chant of squadron names—'Alpha, Alpha, Alpha!' Our seniors had warned us that if our voices dropped, our hands would pay the price later during *ragda*. So, it was better to lose our voices for a day than our arm strength for a week.

The day finally came, and the scene was epic. The boys lined up, shoes tied tighter than our schedules, and faces set with determination. The whistle blew, and we took off like missiles launched on a command. The first few kilometres were a blur of heavy breathing, pounding feet, and the occasional motivational shout. I could have sworn I was in the top twenty. But when I finally grabbed my token—41st!—I looked at it, blinked, and thought, 'Swaran Sahab must have made a mistake,' until I glanced around and saw even more breathless, sweaty faces.

Our senior Saini, Alpha's pride and frontrunner, stormed in the first place, getting his name on the Hodson's Horse board in the mess—a place of honour that every cadet dreams about. The moment you enter the Academy, you think about three boards: the Achievers, the Cross-country Top Finisher, and Appointments.

Our seniors? Absolute legends. The top five spots were taken by them, with our course's best placement being sixth, grabbed by Khassi. The gap between them and us felt like we were trying to race Usain Bolt with a leg cramp.

Post-cross country, the Alpha Squadron was declared the winner, and we were on cloud nine. The buzz was that we had finally secured the champion banner. We celebrated like maniacs. We were so caught up in the euphoria that we completely forgot about school. The warden's temper flared when he found us rushing late, but with a stroke of luck, we managed to reach just in time. Everyone grabbed *paranthas* from the mess, wrapped them in tissue paper, and wolfed them down while sitting on the bus. Picture a group of victorious, half-asleep cadets with *paranthas* hanging out of their mouths—it was a sight to behold.

By the time we got to school, we looked like zombies that had just run a marathon (which, to be fair, we had). The teachers were kind enough to take it easy on us. Some even pretended not to notice when we dozed off during class. By the end of the day, we were back at the Academy, hoping to sneak in a break during evening games. But our PTI, the ever-unpredictable powerhouse, had different plans.

'Five rounds,' he declared with the enthusiasm of a man who hadn't just gobbled down *bhaturas* for lunch. A collective groan rippled through us, but orders were orders. We dragged our sore bodies around the track.

Expecting some mercy after the rounds, we dreamed of playing a gentle game of volleyball. But PTI had a glint in his eye that spelled doom.

'No volleyball! No squash! No lawn tennis! Basketball, football, and hockey only,' he barked. And just like that, we knew it was game over. What followed was a chaotic session of dribbling, sprinting, and yelling that made cross country look like a warm-up.

By nightfall, the Academy had transformed. For the first time, it was quieter than the library during study hours. Everyone was knocked out by 9:30 p.m. The cubicles were full of cadets who, for one rare night, had no strength to talk, joke, or even dream—we were too busy catching up on the sleep we desperately needed.

◆◆◆

The end of the morning parade was something none of us expected. For the first time, there was no usual morning fall-in. Instead, we were ordered to stay in our beds, pretending to study—a move to keep us from catching colds in the chilly weather. But there was one caveat: the door had to stay cracked open just enough for the instructor to peek in during his rounds.

And let's be honest, everyone knows that a man in bed is never fully awake, let alone studying. The Academy's morning silence was legendary—the kind that lulled you back to sleep even if you were trying to keep one eye open. That's exactly what happened when the guard came on his surprise inspection. And Dada, our notorious sleep champion, was caught mid-snore with his book acting as a makeshift pillow. The guard didn't yell or wake him up. Nope—he simply snapped a picture, a silent declaration of doom, and handed it over to the warden as we boarded the bus to school. The outcome? Dada was doomed to face the drill instructor for what could only be described as a 'personalised, bone-cracking fitness session' during the games period.

Ah, and winter—the season of freezing hands and cosy blankets was also the season of cup noodles for us! The best part? No hassle. Just a quick trip downstairs where a camper full of boiling water awaited like a loyal servant. A quick pour into the cup and voilà—instant happiness. Effort level: zero. Satisfaction level: through the roof.

The magic wasn't just in the noodles; it was in the company. Some days, a group of us would gather like an underground noodle cult, huddled together, slurping away in perfect harmony. It wasn't just food; it was an event. I can still picture it—Sariya and I devouring cup noodles every single day for an entire week, thanks to the generous sponsorship of none other than Moan Sahab (our local 'rich man' extraordinaire). Truly, no kettle, no worries, but a camper full of hot water and a rich friend? That's a winter blessing!

School hours were longer due to the winters, meaning we left at 9:00 a.m. in the morning and dragged ourselves back at 3:00 p.m. in the afternoon. And the most feared part? The moment we stumbled into the Academy, expecting a morsel of mercy, we barely completed our lunch, and the orders came: 'Everyone on the track. Five rounds!' The lunch barely had time to settle. It was as if the PTI lived for the thrill of watching us run with '*bhaturas* in the stomach, legs on the track,' and we all knew it.

And then there were the extra-class boys. We pitied them, or maybe they pitied us. By the time they joined us on the track, we were already two laps in, wheezing like old train engines. The boys from the early group, stuffed and slower than molasses in winter, huffed past us, eyes half-closed and stomachs wobbling with each step. '*Arre yaar*, we just got here!' someone whispered, earning a quick side-eye from the PTI, who could somehow hear through the wind.

Those who dared to sneak a glance at their friends exchanged silent, conspiratorial looks that said, 'I'd rather be back in bed pretending to study,' or 'Next time, I'm just going to eat less.'

◆◆◆

A few days later, things were beginning to settle back to normal—or as normal as they could be at the Academy. I was just coming back to my room from the night fall-in, my legs feeling like jelly and my eyes half-closed. The thought of finally getting some sleep was the only thing keeping me moving. I barely had time to flop onto my bed when there was a knock at my door.

'Oh, great. Who's plotting against my sleep this time?' I muttered, dragging myself up. I opened the door to find Rana standing there, looking like he was carrying the weight of the world on his shoulders.

'Shivam,' he whispered, glancing nervously over his shoulder, 'the senior wants you. And me. And, well... Dada and Sooden too.'

'Destiny, thou art cruel,' I thought, my sleepy brain already imagining the worst. I threw on my slippers and trudged out, exchanging wary glances with Rana as we walked to the common room.

The senior sat in his usual throne-like chair, eyes glinting with a mix of amusement and malice. His smile widened as we stood in front of him, a line of doomed soldiers.

'Shivam,' he said, tilting his head with a mock-serious expression, 'I feel like by now, you've learned the lesson from your first stay-back.'

I turned redder than a tomato at a farmer's market. My mind raced: should I say 'yes', 'no', or 'maybe'? Each answer seemed like a one-way ticket to a different kind of trouble.

'Sir... um... yes? No? I mean, yes, sir,' I sputtered, tripping over my words like a new recruit on his first march.

The senior raised an eyebrow and glanced at Sooden. 'Alright, Sooden,' he said, a sly grin forming. 'Chair. Hands on the floor. Legs up.'

Sooden's face dropped, but he obeyed. 'And,' the senior continued, his eyes sparkling with devilish joy, 'with every push-up, you'll give the most melodious... moaning sound.'

A snicker slipped out before I could stop myself. The room was silent for a beat, and then Dada, trying to keep a straight face, was called in to join.

'Dada, you too. Join in.'

The first push-up. '*Aaahnn...*' Sooden started, sounding like a mix between a sleepy bear and a singer who missed the high note. Dada followed with his deep baritone, adding what could only be described as 'the bass line'.

'*Aahnn...*' Dada echoed, the vibration so powerful it felt like the floor shook. I covered my mouth, eyes watering from suppressed laughter.

'Melody! I said melody, not construction work!' the senior barked, but even he couldn't help the chuckle that escaped.

After what felt like an eternity of symphony practice, the senior waved us off. We shuffled back to our rooms, snickering like schoolboys who'd just been let off detention. The first thing I did was find my buddy, GBR.

'GBR,' I sighed dramatically, 'I lost the match. Your mantra couldn't save me this time.' Teasing him for his moaning skills and moan hub victory.

His response? A knowing smile and a pat on the back. In that moment, I knew that no matter what, the Academy's lessons weren't just about discipline—they were about surviving it with a laugh and fun.

Seniors, SSB, and Impact

Bhari sabah mein keh rha hu, yeh AIR 1 lekar aayega!
—Sumit Sir, Impact

Yanking us back into reality, as PT wrapped up, the seniors hit us with a decree—push-ups every night after the fall-in. And trust me, they didn't just tell us; they made sure we were doing them, with one hawk-eyed senior assigned to patrol us like a security camera on Red Bull. Why? Because BPT was coming up again after winter break, and they wanted us to be push-up pros.

One day, I completely spaced out on the night push-ups. I forgot they even existed and made a beeline for MVH to play on the computer, probably trying to conquer some epic level of digital solitaire. Just my luck, one senior discovered my absence and went full detective mode. He ordered the others to drag me back, but before they could nab me, he got sidetracked. Enter Singla's OD. This guy wasn't known for leniency, but he only handed me fifty push-ups and sent me on my way. I knew I'd dodged a bullet—any other senior would've given me a punishment that'd leave me doing push-ups in my dreams.

The next night, I was determined to make up for it. I joined a group of cadets already mid-push-ups when the senior spotted me. '*Oye,* Sharma, *idhar aa*,' he barked. Before I knew it, 'Joban' lifted my legs and placed them on his shoulders like I was a human wheelbarrow. That's right—I was doing elevated push-ups with my legs up in the air. It felt less like exercise and more like a circus act.

Later that night, a game broke out among us—the 'Push-Up Relay Extravaganza'. We split into two teams, each tasked with delivering an object to a senior as fast as possible. My team—Rana, Sooden, and I—took our positions like we were prepping for the Olympics. I was stationed near the water cooler, Sooden at room 24, and Rana way up by room 48. The other team—Joban, Dada, and 'Chawal' (yes, that's right, 'Rice')—took their spots too. It was chaos, it was glory, and in the end, we won. But don't think we escaped unscathed. The seniors set us loose with a laugh that screamed, 'Enjoy your freedom while it lasts,' before shooing us off to our rooms to study.

◆◆◆

NDA Maths classes had kicked off, and let me tell you, they were brutal. Our teacher, dubbed 'Eta' by the seniors (because in AFPI, everything and everyone comes with a legacy nickname), meant business. The moment we got back to our rooms, the air turned from victorious to frantic as everyone scrambled to finish their assignments.

Singla and I, tired of being warriors without caffeine, decided to go rogue for some tea. We trotted to the other block and found Dr DST, our unofficial tea saviour. After a few expertly chosen 'luxury' words, he reluctantly served us that golden nectar. With tea in our veins and a new lease on life, we tackled our assignments, going non-stop until late at night when we finally wrapped up the night's work and collapsed into bed.

Morning came faster than a sneeze, and with it, the 5:00 a.m. alarm. The best part? Not the waking up—definitely not—but the hot coffee and biscuits that awaited us in the mess. The catch? We had to be dressed in full school uniform for NDA Maths classes in the lecture hall, and then straight to the mess for breakfast and then to the school bus.

When we reached school, though, we spotted a new addition—smart TVs in the classrooms. We exchanged looks that said, 'Great, now they can watch us suffer in HD.' But curiosity got the best of us. We went on a covert mission to locate the remote. After a hunt worthy of another Mission Impossible movie, not starring Tom Cruise but us, AFPIans, Lahsun whispered, 'Mission accomplished,' and we fired up some music. It was an impromptu musical night, the whole class vibing to the rhythm—until the door creaked open.

'Oh no, it's Sir!' someone whispered with wide eyes.

Our Maths teacher stormed in like he was auditioning for a role in an action film. 'Are you all out of your minds?' he thundered. 'Using school property for a concert? This isn't MTV!'

We sat there, trying our best to look remorseful, but when he finally left, there was a pause, all of us staring at the door, ensuring sir had truly left, and then, a collective snicker. Moan nudged me and said, 'Hey, at least we were the first ones to use the TV.' And with that, we all broke into laughter, feeling like legends, even if just for a moment.

◆◆◆

Soon after, our seniors began leaving for their SSBs, and life in the Academy took a dramatic turn. With no seniors around to micromanage, it felt like we were birds finally freed from the cage. The corridors were alive with the sound of carefree laughter, and we roamed the Academy in our civil clothes and fancy chappals. Trust me, the swagger was unreal. If you looked closely, you'd probably hear 'Swag se Swagat' playing in the background as we strutted around like Bollywood heroes.

Whenever a senior got recommended, it felt like our own personal victory. As soon as school ended, we'd rush to call their parents using our teachers' phones, asking if they had cleared it. The moment we heard a 'Yes,' it was like Diwali had come early. The sense of pride and happiness was unmatched. Those moments reminded us of why we were here and why every late-night study session, every punishment, and every obstacle was worth it.

However, the joy was short-lived because the recommended seniors soon returned for their practical exams. This meant the fun days were over, and it was time to get back in our shoes as juniors for the last few months,

◆◆◆

By now, a new rule had been imposed—speakers were banned in the Academy. The reason? Apparently, our *dhinchak* songs and late-night DJ sessions were 'disrupting the decorum'. So, all the speakers were confiscated. But you know how every Bollywood movie has one rebel who refuses to comply? That was me. My speaker, cleverly hidden in my room, became a beacon of hope for the entire batch.

'Shivam, speaker *idhar de na, yaar.* Bathroom *mein ek do gane sunna hai,*' one guy would say. Another would show up, whispering, '*Bhai, ek raat ke liye chahiye.* Room *ka* environment set *karna hai.*'

That poor speaker became the ultimate symbol of *samaj seva.* From providing bathroom beats to soothing senti sessions during emotional breakdowns, it did it all. There were times when I'd sit in my room, listening to *Zindagi Na Milegi Dobara* songs, wondering if my life was secretly a movie.

And then came the motivational moments. Watching our seniors hustle through their exams and SSBs was inspiring. Despite the chaos, the laughter, and the occasional madness, we were reminded of the bigger picture. Every time we saw a senior succeed, it fuelled our dreams. We wanted to be them—to wear that uniform with pride and also call our parents one day with the words, 'Mumma, recommend *ho gaya.*'

Through it all, the Academy remained a place of unending chaos, laughter, and life lessons. From tearing pages in Physics files to hiding speakers for survival, every moment added a unique chapter to our story. And as I look back now, I realise that it wasn't just about the punishments or the SSB results. It was about the bonds we formed, the resilience we built, and the memories we created—memories that would stay with us forever.

◆◆◆

The preparation for the arrival of the next junior course was imminent, and the Academy was buzzing like a market during Diwali. The MVH had been locked tighter than a bank's gold vault, protecting the written question papers and answer sheets of the next course where Swaran Sahab stood guard like the Great Gatekeeper of Vaikuntha.

When the written results were declared, a hundred and fifty students were selected for interviews. There it was—the comedy of errors. Some of our coursemates were so determined to find their namesake—or their relatives—on the list, you'd think it was a mission to track family lineage.

The juniors were divided into five batches for the interview process, and soon enough, they started arriving in full force. Along with them came their parents, who carried suitcases, snacks, and, of course, an endless supply of unsolicited advice. While the juniors were busy figuring out where to sit like they were in the middle of a college fest, their parents wandered around the campus like they were on a spiritual pilgrimage. '*Aunty ko dekho, har* tree *ke saath* photo *le rahi hain.* Instagram star *banengi lagta hai!*' someone whispered, eyeing one of the parents who was posing with trees as if she was the latest social media sensation.

Amidst this chaos, our PTI, ever the opportunist, saw the perfect chance to make us pay for the madness. 'Boys!' he roared during what was supposed to be a games period. 'Five rounds of the field—faster than a Shatabdi Express!' and with a whisper, added, 'All the parents are watching; you dare not embarrass me.' We groaned in unison but ran like our lives depended on it. By the end of those rounds, we were gasping harder than a harmonium at full blast. But the PTI wasn't done with his masterpiece yet. 'Now, fifty push-ups. And yes, it's a public performance—show me the best drama!' Parents, meanwhile, were forming their own little audience, watching us like they were at the finals of a kabaddi match.

But the real highlight was the PTI's legendary handstand drill. '*Beta, agar* balance *khoya toh* balance sheet *ban jayegi*,' he warned. As we flipped upside down, sweat dripping down our foreheads, I couldn't help but notice one junior looking at me, wide-eyed and drenched in his own sweat. It was a short break time, and I was sitting on the field, trying to catch my breath. His nervous gaze met mine, and I conveyed, just through my eyes, '*Bhai, yeh toh* trailer *hai.* Picture *abhi baaki hai.*'

Back in the rooms, we gathered in Room No. 1, which had become the unofficial gossip hub of the Academy. We'd lounge around, munching on snacks smuggled in from the canteen, and wait for the chest number announcements. For the next five days, this became our daily ritual—gossip, snacks, and betting on the numbers just by the faces.

The Academy was electric with energy—'High *Josh!*'—and everywhere you turned, something was happening. The PTI would pick the best cadet to shout the slogan loud enough to shake the Himalayas. Between drills, announcements, and the general madness of preparing for the juniors, one thing was crystal clear: this wasn't just a training Academy—it was a battlefield where friendships were forged and memories were made, which would last a lifetime.

The Dual Halls

MVH ka AC bilkul nhi chlega,
apko pta hai Academy ka kitna bill aaya is baar!?
—Warden Sahab

Buried in the heart of the Academy, MVH and PVH were not just rooms; they were institutions in themselves, carrying legacies that every cadet knew about and often feared. MVH, Maha Vir Hall, the cyber cafe, was equipped with ten computers that were supposed to aid in education. But let's be real—education often took a backseat to Instagram scrolling, a few cheeky rounds of solitaire, and, on the luckier days, Counter-Strike tournaments. The catch? You had to dodge the ever-watchful eyes of the staff. If caught by the director, you'd be subjected to his legendary speeches, the kind that started with a thunderous 'YOU THINK YOU'RE SMART?' and ended with your confidence at an all-time low. If a staff member nabbed you, the punishment was more physical—front rolls, frog jumps, or whatever creative torture they could think of on the spot.

Despite its dangers, MVH had its perks. During the sweltering summers, it became a refuge of cold air, a slice of paradise in the midst of relentless training. After dinner, cadets would pile in, sprawling on chairs, basking in the heavenly air-conditioning, briefly forgetting the endless PT sessions and drill routines. For those fleeting moments, MVH felt less like an Academy hall and more like a five-star hotel. But reality hit hard when PTM time rolled around. The same sanctuary turned into a battlefield, where teachers and the director tore into us for every minor infraction, transforming the cool air into a cold reckoning.

On some evenings, after dinner, MVH became the ground for impromptu game sessions. From card games to casual quizzes, it was a place where laughter and camaraderie flourished. These moments, though short-lived, reminded us of the rare simplicity and joy amidst the chaos of Academy life.

Then, there was PVH—Param Vir Hall—the heart of lectures, punishments, and entertainment. It was a hall steeped in tradition and stories. On Sundays, it doubled as a movie theatre, with a lineup heavy on war classics like *Lone Survivor*, *Fury*, *Border*, and the legendary *Saving Private Ryan*. But what made the movie nights unforgettable wasn't just the films—it was the hilarious commentary from the cadets.

During *Fury*, as Brad Pitt's tank roared onto the battlefield, a voice muttered from the back, '*Agar yeh* tank SSB *mein hota, toh* obstacle course *khatam karne ki jagah hum seedha* tank *le jaake* finish line *par* selfie *le lete*!' Another chimed in during a tense standoff scene, '*Agar* Pitt *bhai ne* NDA join *ki hoti, toh* director *se bhi dosti ho jaati*.'

Saving Private Ryan was a favourite. During the Normandy landing scene, as bullets flew and soldiers screamed, a cadet deadpanned, '*Yeh toh kuch bhi nahi hai, hamare* PT parades *zyada* dangerous *hote hain*.' And when Tom Hanks' character delivered his iconic 'Earn this' speech, someone sniffled theatrically, '*Sirf* director *se ek* "good job" *mil jaye, toh hum bhi* earn *kar lenge*.'

The true highlight, however, came when a beautiful female lead graced the screen. The moment she appeared, a wave of murmurs spread across PVH. Heads tilted, grins widened, and someone inevitably whispered, '*Yeh toh* direct heart attack *dene aayi hai.*'

PVH had its own share of peculiar traditions. Whenever seniors came on their rounds during movie screenings, everyone instinctively stood up to greet them with a crisp, 'Good evening, sir.' However, one day, a senior walked in and chuckled, 'Guys, you don't have to stand up in PVH to wish. It's done while sitting in *savdhan*.' A wave of confusion swept over us—how could someone possibly be *savdhan* while sitting? The seniors demonstrated, and soon it became a part of us. This '*baithe baithe savdhan*' position proved surprisingly useful during officer lectures, saving us from unnecessary scoldings and keeping us alert.

PVH wasn't just about movies or scolding cadets. It was also a repository of stories from commissioned officers who returned to share tales of their cadet days. One major, smirking proudly, recalled, '*Tumhe pata hai? Pehle* course *mein galti karte toh bricks uthwate the, construction site ka kaam karwate the. Aur tum log sirf* PT *se thak jaate ho!*' Another senior, unable to contain his laughter, added, '*Aur ek baar gurdwara mein poora* course *raat ko soya tha, kyunki* director *ne poore* seventh-course *ko ek din ke liye* suspend *kar diya tha!*'

In the end, MVH and PVH were more than just halls; they were chronicles of our Academy journey. They taught us to endure, laugh, and find humour in the gravest of moments. Whether it was cooling off in MVH or sharing a laugh over a Brad Pitt joke in PVH, these spaces captured the essence of our life—discipline, resilience, and a whole lot of comedy.

The Festive Celebrations

Yaar, yeh fire extinguisher kaise chalta hai?
—Unknown

Heading into the final stretch, the year was coming to an end, and we, the first years, were finally sent back to our homes. But of course, the holiday wasn't just a regular break—it kept getting extended, thanks to fog and government orders. It felt like we were being sent further and further away from our families and brothers. Missing each other like crazy, we couldn't stop calling each other—group calls, video calls, and all the ways we could connect. We joked around, shared our homesickness, and tried to get through the extended break. But then, finally, the time came to return to the Academy.

And man, it was like we were walking back into the gates of heaven. The excitement was unreal. No one could hold back the joy. As soon as we saw each other, we were slapping backs, high-fiving, and hugging each other. That first moment of reunion was the greatest pleasure, the sweetest feeling of belonging, the rush of being back with the brothers who understood every laugh, every inside joke, and every moment of madness.

And it didn't stop there. A whole lot of surprises were waiting for us, and the first one came in the form of the Lohri celebration. The Academy transformed that day—it was like the whole place came alive. There was music, dancing, and so much energy in the air. But the most mind-blowing part? The interviewing officer and the director—yes, you heard that right—The Director, on the dance floor, vibing with full *josh!*

We were all standing there, eyes wide, thinking, '*Kyun bhai, yeh kaise hua?* Who made them dance?!' It felt like we had witnessed a miracle. These were the men who had their ever-watchful eyes on our backs, who had us marching in lines, who made us sweat through PT and drills—and there they were, dancing in front of us, full of life, grooving like they were at a Bollywood music video shoot.

The whole place erupted with cheers, and for a moment, it felt like everything we'd gone through—every drill, every struggle, every punishment—was worth it just to see this. The director, with his serious face, shaking it to the beat, was the most unexpected, yet hilarious, sight ever. We couldn't stop laughing and clapping.

The day was filled with non-stop fun, great music, and unforgettable moments. It was the kind of celebration that made you forget all the stress, all the discipline, and all the rules of the Academy. It was like being a part of one big, wild family again. A perfect post-break welcome back for us.

◆◆◆

Time flew by so fast, and suddenly, there we were—facing the final exams. The moment of truth, the deciding factor for our new appointments, and the last trial for the championship banner, the test of who would carry the torch forward. But this time, there was a different vibe in the air. A fresh wave of energy was sweeping through the course. Everyone was ready to put their absolute best into the exams.

The exams were like a wildfire—intense and all-consuming. People were burning the midnight oil, fuelled by the endless cups of tea and coffee from Dr DST. And me? Well, I was the self-proclaimed 'supplier of biscuits'. We had everything—tea, coffee, biscuits—and the energy to match.

Exams were rolling on smoothly, or at least, that's what we thought, until Holi came crashing in like a surprise guest just before the last exam. The warden had scheduled some colour festivities for us, but as per the usual hostel chaos, we weren't content with the normal approach. The second the word 'Holi' was mentioned, we took it to the next level.

As the clock struck 12, the entire Academy erupted in a thunderous chorus of 'Happy Holi!' The sound was deafening—horns blaring, kids shouting, and the chaos of a hundred voices combining into a full-on celebration. I was yanked from my deep slumber by the noise, my senses overwhelmed by the commotion. Then, there was a knock on my door. It was Singla, who had just been woken up like me. I barely had time to process what was happening when one of the seniors saw us. He shot an order like a drill sergeant: 'Grab his legs!' And just like that, my coursemates were all over me, dragging me from one end of the squadron to the other, sliding like a penguin on ice. It was a full-on mess, but I couldn't help but laugh at the absurdity of it all.

And let me tell you, the videos we have of that moment are still on our phones. Panda, the warrior of Holi, smiling through the chaos, has become one of those iconic moments we'll never forget. Even though we were all soaked, bruised, and muddied, nothing could kill the spirit of the day.

After the Holi madness came the damage control phase—cleaning time. The SSCs took charge as if it were some military operation. Alpha, on top, sent a flood of water to Charlie; Charlie passed it down to Bravo; and Bravo, stuck at the bottom, was left to clean up the mess. But every now and then, we'd get mischievous and send a wave of water from our bathrooms down, turning Charlie's hard work into a swimming pool. And you could hear them screaming from below, 'What is wrong with you guys?!'

We just stood there, wiping our brows and acting innocent. 'Oops, my bad!'

The sun came up, and even after the unofficial festivities of the night, we weren't done. It was time for a Junior Vs Senior war. The juniors took over the 'A' Block, while the seniors held on to the 'B' Block. Both courses were filling out their buckets, making it our mission to wet the other course. The main hall converted into our battlefield, and the war began.

Now, what else was the perfect time for using the fire extinguisher, which was always placed like some antique showpiece in the Academy? Out came the pin in the extinguishers, and both parties joined in to celebrate.

And then came the official Holi fall-in. As for the colours that were arranged by the warden, well, they were in the air for all of two seconds before we decided it wasn't enough. We then brought in the water bucket to continue the festivities.

But the best part? When we turned on the pipelines and flooded the whole track leading to the basketball ground, it was like a scene straight out of a disaster movie, except we were the heroes of this mess. People were rubbing themselves on the ground, sliding on their elbows, and waddling with their hands on their bums like some weird new form of military training.

And then, just when you thought it couldn't get any crazier—there was a rain of water balloons. Yes, water balloons—gracefully sneaked in by some cadet! From the top room, they came flying down like missiles, hitting everyone in sight. We were all ducking and dodging as if we were on a battlefield. But honestly, we couldn't stop laughing. The entire ground was soaked; everyone was covered in mud, looking like a bunch of warriors.

Then came the drastic moment. One senior, in the heat of the madness, accidentally sprayed water on the director. Cue the silence. We all held our breaths, waiting for him to explode. But... nothing happened. The director just gave us a look, a look of something sinister being plotted in his mind. But that was all. No action. Just a look.

The next day, we had our final English exam, and the course was thinking more about the end of the session than the exam. It was, of course, only the English exam that allowed us the carefree Holi. It was the easiest exam, and honestly, we felt like we were free.

But then, as soon as we stepped off the bus, ready to march into our rooms to pack our bags, things took a turn. Ties were hanging around our necks like we were about to get married, and we were ordered to run straight from the bus to the football ground. But here's the twist—we weren't going for a friendly game of football. No, we had our instructor waiting there to make us do every kind of roll imaginable—front rolls, back rolls, you name it.

And you know what? Our uniforms looked like they had gone through a washing machine—filled with dirt. We all started looking at each other, confused, thinking, 'Should we pack these dirty clothes to show our parents this is what AFPI gives us as a gift for Holi? Or should we just go straight to lunch and act like nothing happened or rest or leave for home?'

But we knew better. It wasn't our course that had anything to do with the incident with the director. That was all on the seniors. We were just the juniors, the ones who had to deal with the aftermath. But at the end of the day, we did what every first-year does—we took our white Mufti, still looking like we had just survived a mudslide, and proudly carried it home. After all, who else could claim to have experienced the luxury of AFPI like us? I mean, if we could survive this, we could survive anything. And that, my friends, was the true gift of AFPI.

And when we finally got home and showed our parents our 'special Holi outfits', they just stared at us like we had walked out of a horror film. But deep down, we knew—we had lived the real Academy experience. And we wouldn't trade it for anything in the world.

Bridges, BMPs, & Beyond

Trip kaisi thi? Kal tak training register mein 500 words!

At AFPI, life was more than just rigorous training; it was a whirlwind of emotions, camaraderie, and unforgettable experiences. Among the highlights of our journey were the visits to military cantonments and air force stations, which gave us a taste of the life we aspired to lead. Each visit was a blend of awe, learning, and laughter—sprinkled with moments that became the stuff of legends.

Our very first outing as juniors was to the Patiala Army Cantonment, and what a day it was! The skies were overcast, and a light drizzle greeted us as we stepped off the bus. But rain? That was no dampener for us! It only added to the thrill as we explored an impressive array of tanks, from T-72s to T-90s. 'Look at these beasts,' someone whispered, and we couldn't agree more. The automatic bridges—engineering marvels that enable rapid troop movements—left us spellbound. And then there were the rifles! Holding an INSAS (Indian Small Arms System) rifle for the first time felt surreal—its weight, its cold metal—as if it carried the history of countless battles.

The demonstrations that followed were mesmerising. Officers walked us through the mechanics of everything from the rifles to LMGs (Light Machine Guns), their precision and discipline captivating us. The day ended with a hearty refreshment spread—*samosas*, *gulab jamun*, and endless cups of tea. 'Sant' (just a saint by name), of course, managed to spill his tea while demonstrating his 'perfect' grip on an imaginary rifle, much to everyone's amusement.

Next on our itinerary was a visit to the Chandigarh Air Force Station. If the Patiala trip was exhilarating, this was nothing short of magical. As we stood before aircraft like the Globemaster, the AN-32, and the Chinook, our aviation dreams took flight. A foreign officer from the Chinook's country of origin gave us a detailed tour of its tandem rotor design and heavy-lift capabilities. 'This is the Boeing CH-47 Chinook,' he explained, and we hung on to every word. PT, not missing a beat, raised his hand and asked, 'Sir, how do you remember so many technical terms?' The officer laughed and said, 'By not trying to interrupt like you do!' The room erupted in laughter, and PT's face turned as red as the flight deck emergency light.

The Military Literature Festival at Sukhna Lake was another gem in our treasure trove of experiences. Meeting decorated officers, including lieutenant generals and brigadiers, left us inspired. One officer shared tales of leading missions in Siachen, emphasising how determination triumphs over physical limits. Gaint, always curious, asked, 'Sir, any funny incidents?' The officer chuckled and recounted how, during a high-altitude mission, a soldier once mistook a heating pad for an instant meal pack and tried to eat it. 'He learned the hard way that not everything in the army comes with instructions!'

We also got our hands on vintage army artefacts, including historical letters and uniforms. In a burst of creativity, we painted a massive AFPI logo on a communal poster with the words 'Long Live AFPI!' It became the centrepiece of the festival, drawing nods of approval from attendees.

Then came the air show at the Sukhna on the occasion of Air Force Day—a spectacle we'll never forget. The Suryakiran Aerobatics Team painted the sky with tricolour streaks, their formations leaving us awestruck. On the way back, we convinced the driver to stop for street food. *Samosas*, *pakoras*, and bottles of Cola became the perfect ending to an extraordinary day.

Our final major outing was to Zirakpur Cantonment, where we experienced the thrill of riding a BMP (an infantry fighting vehicle). The vehicle's rugged movements had us clinging on for dear life, laughing hysterically as it bounced and swerved across the field. Cadets held on for their dear lives to anything they could get a hold of and tried not to fall off it.

The floating bridge walk was another adventure. As it swayed gently with every step, Moan, ever the dramatist, declared, 'If I fall, tell my story!'—a statement met with a chorus of, 'No one's writing that long!' Officers' lectures about cantonment life and the camaraderie among soldiers left a lasting impression, reminding us why we chose this path.

These visits were more than just outings; they were lessons, bonding moments, and endless sources of laughter. Each experience brought us closer as cadets and reaffirmed our commitment to the dream we all shared.

Adios Amigos

Juniors chote bhai hote hai, chote bhai!
—Warden Sahab

In a grand display, the farewell of our seniors started with us giving them the send-off they deserved. The school organised multiple events, activities, and a massive lunch that included both seniors and us. Even the other Shemrockites, ones we usually never much interacted with, joined in, making it feel like one big celebration. The best part? The teachers showing off their moves on the stage.

Then came the grand farewell from our side. We planned a memorable evening for our seniors, starting with Singla and me as hosts—your very own Manish Paul and Kapil Sharma. And the preparation we all had put in as a course was legendary. Every cadet contributed whatever they could; the localites got the mementoes made, we got our own version of disco lights for the dance performances, and whatnot.

The first game? The legendary 'Incognito Personality' challenge. The most original idea we both could come up with. It was time to test how much our seniors really knew about the world. Let's just say one senior nailed it so hard that we almost started calling him 'Chrome Bhai'.

Next came the titles. Oh, the fun we had! There was 'Mr Casanova', 'Mr AFPI', 'Mr PT', and my personal favourite, 'Mr Bakchod'. The mementoes we prepared, personalised 'Double Firsts' T-shirts were then presented by us, something our seniors then wore till their end of days.

We weren't done yet. The treasure hunt we organised became pure chaos. To get their clues, the seniors had to earn them—*ragda* time! Push-ups, sprints, and some classic PTI drills were the price for each hint. '*Arrey,* clue *ke liye itna bhaag rahe ho jaise* pizza delivery *ka* timer *lag gaya hai*!' Watching them run from one spot to another like contestants on Khatron Ke Khiladi was priceless. The competition was fierce, but their spirit? Unquestionable.

Then came the pièce de résistance: cake cutting. By the time we gathered, I noticed something alarming—no refreshments were left! Singla and I looked at each other. '*Arrey bhai, lagta hai hum apne* share *ka* entertainment *pee gaye!*' But no regrets—the seniors' joy was worth it.

Dinner turned into the ultimate bonding moment. For the first time ever, the mess hall was packed—juniors and seniors eating together. Usually, it's 'juniors *pehle,* seniors *baad mein*' because, well, hierarchy. But that night? Full-on 'unity in diversity' vibes.

The grand finale? Our surprise dance performance. And trust me, the '*Haye Garmi*' step lit up the floor. Seniors cheered like crazy; some even joined in. By the end, we weren't just cadets and seniors anymore; we were a family. It wasn't just a farewell—it was an evening to remember, filled with jokes, sweat, and memories for a lifetime AFPI style—full *josh* and double *bakchodi*!

The final weeks passed, and came the Passing Out Parade (POP)—the grand finale, the emotional rollercoaster, and, for one senior, the ultimate meltdown moment. This was the guy who never flinched, never broke a sweat, and once did two-hundred push-ups while we struggled with ten. But there he was, bawling like a kid who just lost his candy.

Just then, our drill instructor—whose stare could make even Gabbar Singh tremble—noticed him. He strode over and said, '*Arrey, kya kar raha hai? Teri* girlfriend *ne chod diya?* Control yourself! Academy *ke bahar aur bhi bada rona milega, jab* EMI *bharni padegi!*'

The room erupted in laughter. Even the senior wiped his tears, laughing through his sniffles. 'Sorry, sir. No more crying,' he managed to say, standing up straighter. The instructor, not one to let things slide, added with a smirk, '*Bas theek hai. Lekin agli baar* tissue box *leke aana.*'

With that, the POP turned into a mix of crying and comedy. It was a moment to remember—tears, laughs, and lessons in resilience, all wrapped into one.

As the evening progressed, the official awards were distributed by the director. Titles like 'Best All-Round Cadet', 'Best in Drill', 'Best in Academics', and 'Best in PT and Sports' were handed out with pride. While everyone clapped enthusiastically, we juniors had our eyes on one thing: the motivational speeches. They started well—full of life lessons and big dreams—until the principal took the mic.

Now, let me paint you a picture. Our principal was known for trying a little too hard to speak the Queen's English. As she announced the 'Best in Academics', she confidently referred to the chairman as 'Chair-Moan'. The hall went silent for a moment before someone snickered, and then the laughter exploded within us. For the rest of the year, 'Chair-Moan' became an inside joke.

But wait, there's more. This wasn't the first time our principal unintentionally brought the house down. During the sports meet earlier that year, she grabbed the mic and said, 'Am I audible? If yes, raise your hands.' Nobody moved. She paused, then said, 'Okay, let me move forward. Maybe you'll hear me better there.' We sat there thinking, 'Madam, speaker *ka* problem *hai, aapka nahi!*' But who could correct her? After all, she was the principal, and principals are meant to be followed—especially when they have a mic.

The POP ended with us shouting the legacy 'Eleventh Course *ki Jai Ho*' slogan while our seniors slowly marched, donning the AFPI

Khaki for one last time. We, with full *josh*, cheered them on, ready to say our goodbyes.

The day soon came when our seniors started leaving, and, to be honest, I never expected it to hit me like it did. I mean, my OD and I never really had a connection, but on the last day, something changed. I was in my room, lost in the usual chaos, when he called me downstairs.

It felt weird, like an unwelcome distinction. We had spent an entire year with them, and now it seemed like something had been taken from us—like the bond we'd built would never be the same again. But what could we do? We were the seniors now. The official head was always the staff.

I came downstairs, past the water cooler, and there he was—my OD—Alex Sir, waiting for me. I still remember his words so clearly. 'Bro,' he said, 'I know I'm leaving, and I couldn't help you much, but I want you to know—that this place itself is enough to teach you a lifetime of lessons. Remember, you are an AFPIan. No matter what happens, you never break. If you ever need anything—help, advice, or just a favour—don't hesitate. Dial my number. I've got your back.'

And then, we shared a man hug—a moment so real that it felt like a brother was leaving behind a pair of shoes I could never hope to fill.

At that moment, I felt something I hadn't really understood before—like a switch had flipped. I recalled what one of the officers, an AFPIan, had said to us earlier: 'Each of you is a senior and junior while you're in the Academy, but the moment you leave these gates, you're all brothers. May be older, may be younger, but always brothers. You'll always be there for each other, no matter what.'

That hug from my OD wasn't just the gesture of a senior. As he pulled away, he placed a hand on my shoulder and said, 'If a man is destined to fail, let him at least fail in pursuing what he truly desires.' I kept my emotions in check, but his words resonated deeply within me. It wasn't just advice—it was a reminder to follow my path, no matter the outcome.

As I stood there, feeling the weight of his words, I realised that this wasn't just about leaving a building or a room. It was about leaving behind the kind of bond that will always stay with you, no matter where life takes you. That day, I didn't just say goodbye to a senior. I said goodbye to someone who had taught me more than any textbook ever could. And at that moment, I learned that no matter where we went from there, we weren't alone. We had ***AFPI and AFPIans.***

TERM II

THE GLORY

For the Titans of Twelfth
May Our Legacy Live Forever!

46 Men

Oye BCC, Director se Liberty ke liye puch!

It was a relief as the junior term officially ended and the senior term began, with the Term II batch now on our collars. We were no longer the underdogs—we were stepping into the shoes of leaders, the gods of our little AFPI nation. But before all that, we were granted a two-day break after the eleventh-class examinations. For the local cadets, it was business as usual, but for outstation guys like me, it felt like a blink-and-you-miss-it holiday.

As we returned to the Academy, some of us carried our 'boots' with newfound confidence. We were seasoned now, and no guard at the AFPI gates could even dream of catching us slipping. A few days later, the results of the eleventh class were announced. While twenty-four guys initially qualified for the prestigious Torch, our director, with his signature smirk, dropped the hammer. He announced that the Torch would now be awarded based on the combined results of the half-yearly and final exams. The list shrank faster than a new cadet's ego during *ragda*—down to a solid eight.

My buddy and Singla missed the Torch by a hair—just 0.4%! I, on the other hand, barely held onto my dignity with a humble 75%. During the post-results pep talk, the drill instructor praised our course, calling it the best he'd seen in his twelve-year career at the Academy. 'This is the most academically and physically fit course in AFPI history!' he declared. But while the room beamed with pride, I sat there feeling like the odd one out.

Also, for the first time in 12 years, the Alpha Squadron had made history. The Bravo Championship streak was broken, and Alpha was crowned the champions. Now, being the champion squadron came with its own perks, boasting rights, of course, and also, unlike the other squadrons, we wore our Drill Test Lanyard on the right side, showcasing us as champions.

Meanwhile, PT was already in full swing. The BPT after winter PT break was nothing less than a record. The Titans, as we proudly called ourselves, cleared the higher running standards with ease. Everyone completed the 2.4 km run in under ten minutes! Even the PTI couldn't hide his joy, and he walked around grinning like he'd just won the lottery. He even shared his notorious plan of failing a few coming in at the borderline time, which failed miserably as we had all closed in a minute early.

Then came the big moment—the declaration of appointments. It was a dramatic ceremony, with an aura of anticipation so thick you could slice it with a bayonet. When the names were finally announced, the nicknames that followed had us in splits:

BCC (Battalion Cadet Captain): Gaint – 'The towering titan of academics and PT!'

BCA (Battalion Cadet Adjutant): Bakra – 'The "sacrificial goat" of study hours, but hey, the grades spoke for themselves!'

SCCs (Squadron Cadet Captains):

Alpha SCC: Khassi – 'Don't let the name fool you—tough as nails, he could silence a room with one glare.'

Bravo SCC: Kansal – 'Known for his massive appetite, but equally massive discipline.'

Charlie SCC: Joban – 'The dude who made PT look like a walk in the park—literally.'

The ***CSMs (Cadet Sergeant Majors)*** were equally iconic:

Alpha CSM: Sooden – 'A true multitasker, leading from the front while planning pranks like a pro.'

Bravo CSM: Balli – 'The silent killer—quiet but deadly in execution and a man of gym or maybe laundry too.'

Charlie CSM: Bhoru – 'The guy with jokes so bad, they could make a PTI faint, but his drill was flawless.'

Lastly, the ***CQMSs (Cadet Quarter Master Sergeants),*** aka the mess havildars, were crowned:

Alpha CQMS: Rana – 'The self-proclaimed king of food inspections and a fall-in on time always man.'

Bravo CQMS: Gyani – 'A walking encyclopaedia with a side of sass, and when lights are gone, he is on.'

Charlie CQMS: NSG – 'Silent but lethal, just like the commando force he was nicknamed after.'

Even as we cheered for our buddies, we knew in our hearts that most of these appointments wouldn't last the session. But for now, it was celebration time—every achievement felt like our own.

◆◆◆

It was a lazy Saturday morning, and the Academy was unusually calm. The calm before the storm, perhaps, because the next day, the juniors were set to arrive. And with them, a new hierarchy of power would be born—we, the seniors, were ready to reign supreme. Alpha SCC, our self-appointed 'Understudy Distributor-in-Chief', had the important duty of matching us seniors with our rightful undies.

Around eight, I was in my personal sanctuary—the bathroom. It was one of those rare moments when I allowed myself some peace and shampoo-induced reflection. Suddenly, I heard an obnoxiously loud knock on my door with the SCC declaring himself.

'Oi, SCC! *Kya chahiye, bhai*? I'm in the shower!' I shouted back, expecting the decent thing to happen—a bit of patience. But this was AFPI, and patience was as alien as Moan's presence in the mess.

The knocking grew louder, almost rhythmic, like a tribal drumbeat of war. My door had a peculiar quirk: hit it at the right angle, and it would pop open. And, of course, SCC Alpha knew this all too well. BAM! The door swung wide open, and I sprang into action, wrapping myself in the towel as fast as I could and rushing to the door.

Standing there with his signature mischievous grin, SCC Alpha Khassi looked like he'd won the lottery. His smirk screamed I'm here to ruin your morning. 'Bro,' I said, clutching my towel like it was a lifejacket, 'What's so urgent you've got to break down my door?'

'Understudy selection,' he announced grandly as if he were distributing awards.

'Bro, seriously? While I'm in the shower?' I glared at him, hoping my death stare would scare him off. But Khassi was Khassi. He tried to step inside like a landlord inspecting his property.

Then came the worst moment. His eyes darted to my towel, and I knew that look—that evil, towel-snatching look. 'Khassi, I swear, if you even think about—' I couldn't finish. He lunged for the towel. Chaos erupted.

What followed was a bizarre tug-of-war. Him pulling, me holding on for dear life. Shampoo was getting in my eyes, my balance was shaky, and I was one step away from public embarrassment. 'Khassi! *Bhai*, leave it! If this towel drops, so help me, you won't live to see your understudy!'

Just when I thought I'd lose the battle (and my dignity), he let go. I stumbled back, panting, and glared at him. 'Now, will you tell me why you're here before I murder you?'

'Pick your understudy,' he said nonchalantly as if the previous scene hadn't happened.

'In this condition? Seriously?' I gestured at my towel-clad self.

'Bro, do it fast. Or the good ones will be gone.'

'Okay, fine. Give me Heera,' I said, trying to mask my growing irritation.

'Heera? Taken by me,' Khassi replied with a smug grin, adding a dramatic 'Hehehehe' like a cartoon villain.

'Alright then, Aniket?'

'Gone.'

'Fine, give me some Sharma. There's got to be one left.'

'Sharma? Gone too. Popular name, bro,' he said, nodding like he was discussing stock market trends.

'Okay, what about Dhiman? Sounds solid.'

'Already taken. Great taste, huh?'

I threw my hands up in exasperation. 'Bro, what did you leave for me? The guy who is not going to join us here?'

Khassi let out a laugh so loud it echoed down the corridor. 'Pretty much, but you are still left with nine options.'

By now, my patience was as thin as my towel. I rubbed shampoo out of my eyes and grumbled, 'Okay, no turbaned guys. I can't teach them how to wear it properly. It's better for everyone.'

He rolled his eyes. 'Bro, your logic is as lame as my jokes.'

Speaking of lame jokes, he added, 'You know, very few people get to pick their understudy while wearing undies or may be just a towel.'

He cackled at his own joke while I stared at him deadpan. 'Khassi, that was worse than the principal's Queen's English.'

Finally, I noticed two similar names on the list: Paramdeep and Paramraj. 'Give me Paramdeep,' I said decisively.

'Done. Welcome your new understudy—Cadet Paramdeep Singh—617/A/13,' he said, scribbling it down.

Relieved, I closed the door, but not before Khassi made one last attempt at snatching my towel. This time, I was quicker. I slammed the door shut, but not before the towel got caught in the frame. I stood there, defeated yet victorious, holding onto the door with one hand and my dignity with the other.

Paramdeep—my new understudy. His success (or failure) was now tied to me. If he screwed up, I'd be the one on the receiving end of the wrath. And knowing my luck, that was almost guaranteed.

Still, I had hope. Maybe, just maybe, this would be the beginning of a decent OD-undy relationship. Or maybe it'd just be the beginning of a new nightmare. Only time would tell.

◆◆◆

After the Academy appointments, the season of school appointments was upon us, and AFPI was all set to flex its mettle. When it came to the head boy position, everyone already knew who'd snag it—Guruji. Even the teachers pretended to conduct interviews for appearances, but everybody knew that the decision was already made.

A panel was set up: the principal, coordinator, sports in-charge, school psychologist, and others. Guruji strolled in confidently like a king entering his court. Five minutes later, he was officially the head boy.

Next came the house captain selections, and our squad didn't disappoint. Doda took charge of Harvard, and Chawal took over Stanford. Meanwhile, I had my own moment of glory, being chosen as the editor. Frankly, I was just lucky that 'Thakur'—the Shakespeare of our batch—wasn't competing.

'You're an editor?!' Doda teased. 'Let me know when you need help rhyming cat with hat.'

'Sure,' I shot back, 'right after you figure out how to shave off that caterpillar you call a moustache!'

Speaking of which, Doda had a bet with Lahsun that if he became house captain, he'd shave his moustache. Now, Doda, being Doda, was trying to weasel out. He locked himself in Guruji's room bathroom, but Lahsun wasn't about to let him off. Armed with a cockroach spray and a can of deodorant, Lahsun began fumigating the bathroom like a pest exterminator.

'*Bachao! Bachao!* I'm dying!' came Doda's muffled screams from inside.

Outside, Lahsun chuckled. 'Come out, "Captain Caterpillar", or I'm turning up the heat!'

While this chaos unfolded, I was engaged in my own battle with NSG over a speaker.

'Bro, just give me the speaker!' he insisted.

'No way! I'm using it first!'

'Fine, but don't blame me when your playlist starts playing nursery rhymes.'

Eventually, I surrendered the speaker. Sweaty now, I planned to have a bath, so I stripped down to my underwear, and thirst hit me. So, in undies, I marched to my saviour, Guruji's Room 17, and asked, 'Guruji, could you fill my water bottle? I'm too lazy to dress.'

But just as I was basking in my rebellion, he arrived. The storm we called Atma Sahab. The room went silent as he entered.

'Everyone out!' he barked.

'But sir, it wasn't our—'

'OUT!'

I was caught standing in the corner, trying to blend into the shadows. His eyes locked onto me.

'You. To the PT area. Now!'

'Sir, I'm not even dressed—'

'NOW!'

After a lot of begging, he finally let me change into my PT gear. Down at the ground, he lined us up for frog jumps.

'Link arms like a train,' he ordered.

Doda, ever the comedian, whispered, 'Sir, can we add a horn to this train?'

We all glared at him, silently promising revenge for that comment.

Then, Atma Sahab scanned the group.

'Where's "Lambu"?' he demanded.

Lambu, the tall beanpole of our squad, was hiding upstairs, probably shaking like a leaf.

Atma Sahab marched off to retrieve him.

Meanwhile, we were frog-jumping towards Block 'B', a sacred territory of juniors. The humiliation was unbearable. 'Sir, can't we turn back?' someone dared to ask.

'No! Keep going!' came the reply.

Just as we reached the Block 'B' corridor, Atma Sahab turned around and declared, 'This is your warning.' We sighed in relief and returned to our rooms. Doda finally shaved his moustache, and for a moment, we saw his big upper lip for the first time in years.

Soon, it was time to welcome the juniors. Suddenly, we were the ones in charge, the ones they'd look up to (or fear). Divided into companies now, we knew our paths might not always cross, but one thing was certain: we were the seniors.

As we stood on the threshold of our senior term, a strange mix of pride and responsibility filled the air. The days of survival were behind us. Ahead lay the task of leading and, let's be honest, a whole lot of fun at their expense.

Arrival of the Tigers

STUDDDD Bhaiii, ladki se baat kr rha.

Long-awaited, the day finally arrived—the first-ever special prayer in the school auditorium. Hosting it felt like a big deal, especially since I was sharing the stage with the head girl of the school, Diksha. Over the past weeks of preparation, we'd become friends, but let me tell you, this friendship came with its own set of dramas.

Every time she came to my class to fetch me for preparation, it felt like a scene straight out of a Bollywood movie. My classmates would lose their minds.

'Oh, Shivam! *Tere din toh* set *hain*!' they'd yell, grinning ear to ear.

Another one would pipe up, 'Bhai, what's the secret? Share your skills, bro!'

I'd roll my eyes. 'It's for work, you fools. There's nothing else to it.' But the teasing never stopped.

Even our Maths teacher got in on the action one day. 'Shivam, is there something we should know?'

'No, sir! It's just… school duty,' I stammered, feeling the heat rise in my cheeks.

Meanwhile, Diksha would stand there, arms crossed, unimpressed. 'Can we go now?'

Finally, the big day arrived. The stage lights came on, and the event began. For a few minutes, everything was going smoothly.

As the names were announced, I noticed something that flipped my mood entirely. Among the 30 awardees, more than 15 were AFPIans! Suddenly, it wasn't just about hosting; it was about cheering for them.

'Diksha, it's my mates!' I whispered, practically bouncing on the spot.

'Great. Just don't embarrass us,' she replied, exasperated.

And then, disaster struck—the mic cut out. But did that stop me? Nope. I cupped my hands and shouted, 'Let's go, AFPI!' loud enough to echo through the auditorium.

'Shivam! Keep it professional!' Diksha scolded, but even she couldn't hide her smile.

The ceremony ended with applause, and as I walked back into my class, my friends were ready with their commentary.

'So, Shivam, hosting with the head girl, huh? What's next? Are you running for school president?'

I groaned. 'It's called teamwork, you clowns. Ever heard of it?'

◆◆◆

The room reshuffling saga began when the new block assignments were announced. Seniors moving to the 'A' (Alpha) Block were on a mission—'Take the best, leave the rest.' Armed with this unspoken code, we descended upon the 'B' (Bravo) Block like seasoned looters. Mattresses, chairs, cushions—if it spelt comfort, it was ours. Mau summed it up best, clutching his pillow dramatically: 'Why should we suffer just because they're new?'

Balli, however, decided to go a step further. He insisted on dragging his ancient drawer from the 'B' Block to the 'A' Block, a piece of furniture so fragile it felt like it might crumble at the sound of a sneeze. As he staggered along the corridor, someone quipped, '*Bhai*, this drawer is older than our warden's rules.' By the time he reached the 'A' Block, the drawer looked ready to give up on life entirely, wobbling so pathetically that even the termites seemed to have second thoughts about it.

Meanwhile, I was busy relocating my things from Room 34 to 32. The rooms may sound close, but they were a floor apart. Mau, true to form, refused to lift a finger. 'Are you trying to turn me into a labourer?' he protested. Naturally, I ended up shifting his belongings from Room 32 to 10 while he supervised with the authority of a construction site manager.

Balli, not one to miss the theatrics, was hauling motivational posters to his new room. 'If the walls aren't inspiring, the room isn't mine!' he declared, to which someone yelled, 'If the room isn't clean, the room belongs to Mau!' and I could definitely agree with it.

The real highlight, though, was Chawal's almirah crisis. His new Room 40 lacked one, sparking Operation Almirah Transfer. I, Atma Sir, Balli, and Chawal teamed up to move an almirah from Room 60 to 40. What ensued was nothing short of a military drill. At one point, Balli, sweating like a furnace, gasped, 'Stop, stop! I think the almirah's winning this battle!' By the time we got it into Room 40, we felt less like seniors and more like commandos who'd just relocated an arsenal.

To top it all off, the block changes introduced new rules. We were too tired to care, though, especially after spending the entire night and half of the morning shifting rooms. The corridors were a chaotic maze of mattresses and trunks, with exhausted us slumped in corners. Mau, observing the mess, declared grandly, 'One thing's clear—comfort first, juniors later.'

Finally, salvation arrived in the form of the new special breakfast at Manekshaw Mess: coffee with pav bhaji. After our Herculean efforts, it felt like a five-star meal. As we devoured the food, 'Rishi' (really like his name) took a bite and sighed, 'This *pav bhaji* tastes better than Liberty!' We couldn't help but laugh, knowing full well that the chaos of the upcoming day, with the juniors arriving and school resuming, was just around the corner.

◆◆◆

It was finally the moment we had all been eagerly waiting for—the juniors' arrival. As the sun rose, the SCCs were given orders to oversee the process. The Academy was bustling with parents and fresh recruits, all clueless about the trials that awaited. Parents were busy ensuring their 'kids' settled in smoothly, while appointments were tasked with guiding them through the labyrinth of admission verifications and documentation.

As the day progressed and the parents left, the real fun began. With the fresh recruits now on their own, the SCCs were dispatched to the 'B' Block to teach them the basics: how to settle down, organise their rooms, bedsheets, squadron sheet, almirah layout and—most importantly—the art of respect.

Khassi was quick to express his frustration. 'Bro,' he said, 'it feels like your understudy doesn't even know how to give respect to a senior.'

I couldn't help but laugh. 'Bro, he just arrived! You're already expecting him to bow down and call you "Sir"?'

Khassi, however, was serious. 'Still, man! This is the Armed Forces. There's no such thing as "*bhaiya*". It's all "Sir".'

It was clear that Khassi was itching to hear someone address him as 'Sir'. He'd been dreaming of this moment for months, and his patience was running thin. We all laughed it off, knowing we'd soon get our moment of glory.

Our laughter turned into outright hilarity when the director came around for his daily inspection. One of the juniors, clueless about protocol, walked straight up to him and said, 'Uncle, my flush isn't working.'

The director, trying to suppress his laughter, later shared the story with us. 'The ones you're expecting respect from don't even know who the director is yet!' he said, chuckling. That comment became the joke of the year. But we never got the chance to know who the junior was.

◆◆◆

The evening brought the much-anticipated introduction session. For this, we had planned something special. Tatyaal, our unofficial 'master of ceremonies', was chosen to introduce us to the juniors. Standing tall and proud, he began:

'Good evening, juniors. Welcome to the Alpha Squadron. Here, you will learn discipline, courage, and the true meaning of camaraderie. But first, let me introduce you to the legends you'll be calling "Sir" from today.'

'This is your SCC. The guy with more *josh* in him than the combined energy of the entire Academy! If you ever feel low, just look at his face. You might think he's angry, but trust me, it's pure enthusiasm.'

The SCC interrupted with a smirk, 'Juniors, you better call me Sir with pride and remember, I'm not here to babysit you. But… if you survive under me, you'll thank me later. Until then, fall in line!'

He continued, 'This is our CSM, Sooden, our PT stud. If you think you can beat him in a push-up contest, think again.'

He turned to me. 'This is Sharma, our resident poet and writer. If you ever need a speech, a poem, or a heartfelt letter to your girlfriend back home, he's your man.'

I nodded, playing along. 'I charge extra for love letters,' I quipped, earning a round of laughter.

Tatyaal continued, 'This is Singla, our walking, talking Kindle. If there's a book you are thinking of reading, he's already read it twice. Juniors, if you ever feel like broadening your horizons—or pretending to impress someone—ask him for book recommendations. But beware, his suggestions come with a side of unsolicited wisdom!'

The introductions continued with more colourful descriptions:

– 'Meet Guruji, the academic genius. He solves Math problems faster than you can spell calculus.'

– 'This is Thakur—a gym enthusiast with unmatched football skills, a knack for poetry, and a heart that speaks in *shayaris*.'

– 'And here's "KG", our football star. If he's not scoring goals, he's scoring… well, let's just say he's a popular footballer.'

Lastly was Tatyaal himself. 'And yours truly,' he said, 'the best swimmer in the Academy. If you're drowning in the pool—or in life—I'll pull you out.'

Then, it was the juniors' turn to introduce themselves. We had decided on a few standard questions to make things interesting—'What's your name?', 'Where are you from?', and 'What's one thing you're good at?'

One by one, they replied nervously.

– 'I'm Sharma from Ropar. I… um… I'm good at… uh… studying?'

'Studying? We'll see about that,' Lahsun joked.

– 'I'm Dhiman from Pune. I play the guitar.'

'Great! You'll be our entertainment during punishment hours,' Sooden said, earning a round of laughter.

Then, one standing at last was asked what he was good at, and he stammered, 'I… I don't know, Sir.'

'Don't worry,' Dada said. 'By the time we're done with you, you'll be good at everything.'

When my understudy's turn came, he stood confidently and introduced himself: 'Sir, my name is Paramdeep. My father is an ex-serviceman, and I am a gymnast and an artist.' Before the applause could settle, Dada quipped, 'Oh, so you must be as flexible as Nora Fatehi!' The stage erupted in laughter, and he turned redder than a tomato.

Before he could respond, Mushki added with a grin, 'We'll see how smooth your moves are in the anteroom later!' And the teasing didn't stop.

As the warden finally arrived, the announcement to disperse came as a relief to juniors and a challenge for us. 'Back to your rooms, gentlemen,' he declared, reminding everyone of the school day ahead. The BCC promptly echoed the command, dismissing us like a well-rehearsed orchestra.

We trudged back to our rooms, adjusting to the peculiarities of our 'new normal'. It wasn't long before we spotted a few juniors, eager and wide-eyed, rushing to cater to every whim of the seniors. Some carried water bottles like they were delivering holy nectar, while others fanned seniors with files as if they were emperors. It was a scene straight out of our own first-day flashbacks, though no one dared intervene. After all, everyone has their own way of dealing with first-day nerves—or earning blessings.

But something was different this year. The Alpha Block was sealed off, with guards stationed outside the anteroom. 'It feels like a jail upgrade!' someone remarked. The block was sealed like Fort Knox. The connecting bridge and upper-floor doors were locked tight, a new layer of mystery added to our already unpredictable lives. It was quite the contrast from our first days, where everything from the doors to the bridges was wide open, almost inviting mischief.

As we settled back into our rooms, rearranging uniforms and personal chaos, reality hit hard. Our schedules loomed like a ticking clock: impact classes, PT, school, and games—an unending cycle of chaos and discipline. Meanwhile, the juniors were bound to face the ultimate challenge tomorrow: making it to school on time.

◆◆◆

For us, it was just another day, racing to school at 7:20 a.m. sharp. But the juniors? They were about to discover the sacred art of 'speed dressing', or a smaller version of *putti parade* likely accompanied by a generous dose of shouting and panicking. We couldn't help but chuckle at the impending chaos. Little did they know, their crash course in survival had just begun.

After dinner that day, the anteroom was buzzing as unusual, a hotspot for juniors to showcase their 'talents'. It was their moment to shine—or embarrass themselves in ways that would be talked about for weeks. On that particular evening, couples were pairing up for dance routines that had everything—drama, energy, and just a hint of cringe. We were just missing a Bollywood director yelling, 'Cut! Perfect take!'

After dinner, as I was strolling outside, Sariya stormed towards me, grinning from ear to ear.

'Shivam, bro! You missed it!' he exclaimed, his voice dripping with excitement.

'Missed what?' I asked, already suspicious of his enthusiasm.

'Your understudy! That guy lit up the stage!'

I raised an eyebrow. 'Wait, my understudy? What did he even do?'

Sariya could barely contain himself. 'Bro, I'm telling you, he's the next Nora Fatehi! His *Haye Garmi* performance? LEGENDARY. Even the juniors who were standing outside rushed in to watch him.'

I blinked. '*Haye Garmi?* My understudy? Are you sure we're talking about the same person?'

Sariya clapped his hands dramatically. 'Bro, you've got no idea. First, he started with the classic belly roll—except it looked like he was trying to shake off ants crawling on his stomach. Then he did this helicopter arm spin, where he almost knocked over another junior.'

I couldn't help but laugh. 'What else did he do?'

'Oh, the best part was his finale: the *nagin* step combined with the moonwalk. Picture a snake trying to glide backwards—pure comedy gold! The crowd went wild. Even the guys chilling near the mess stopped eating to cheer for him.'

By now, a few juniors had gathered around us, overhearing the conversation. One of them chimed in, 'Sir, he's not lying. Your understudy legit killed it! He's got moves!'

Another junior added, 'Sir, that belly roll was so intense, I thought he might roll off on me.'

I shook my head, trying to process it all. 'I need to see this guy dance. Tomorrow, I'm making him recreate the whole thing.'

'Good luck, bro,' Sariya said, smirking. 'But don't blame me if he outshines you on stage.'

As I walked back to my room, I couldn't stop laughing. It wasn't just about the dancing—it was about the sheer madness of it all. In the anteroom, juniors were still re-enacting parts of the performance, shouting, '*Haye Garmi!*' and mimicking the belly roll.

Shaking The Ground

Do you think you are fuckin' gods!?
—Director Sahab

On the dot of 5:50 in the morning, the hooter blared, marking the first PT for the Tigers. True to tradition, they lived up to the legendary lateness associated with rookies. While the twelfth course stood polished and ready for prayer, the thirteenth course was still scrambling to assemble, some with bed hair that seemed untouched by water.

By five-fifty, they finally stumbled into formation, looking like they'd been dragged from their beds by force, and justice came swift and rolling—literally. About six or seven juniors found themselves flopping into front rolls, and it was clear that most of them had no clue what they were doing. Some spun like a crooked wheel, others looked like turtles on their backs, and one managed to roll in one place as if he'd hit an invisible wall.

The sight was so ridiculous that even Dada cracked a grin before whispering, 'If this is rolling, you better start practising crawling!'

And then came Dada's prayer chant—a performance so thunderous that it could rival a rock concert. The juniors, visibly clueless, resorted to the ultimate rookie tactic: lip-syncing. 'Mmmmm,' they hummed in unison, with mouths moving like broken puppets. Their effort to blend in was so bad that even the seniors had to stifle their laughter.

Once the prayer wrapped up, Rajinder Sahab took the report with his signature seriousness. For the Alpha group (all of Alpha and half of Charlie), it was time for drill—preparing for the dreaded Drill Square Test (DST). Swaran Sahab's pep talk echoed in our heads: 'Everyone must make it in the first go!' The Bravo group, meanwhile, had PT (Bravo and the other half of Charlie). The juniors? They were handed over to Atma Sahab for a 'light' initiation run. 'One minute running, five minutes walking,' he announced with a straight face, earning a few sighs of relief. A modest 3 km awaited them, which felt like nothing to us.

By the time the Bravo group returned from their 5 km run—battle-hardened after sets of push-ups, sit-ups, toe touches, and chin-ups—the juniors were still wobbling in. They were a mix of relief and agony, huffing and puffing as if they'd just survived a marathon. 'First flight? More like the first flop,' Mau quipped, earning a round of chuckles.

Each of us was fully determined to prove our discipline to the juniors that day. Even Husan and Rana, the usual latecomers, were on time. In my haste to get ready, I managed to nick myself while shaving—right near my ear. Blood gushed out as if I'd fought a duel, but I had no time to deal with it. I slapped on some powder to camouflage the disaster and hoped it would pass for a war wound.

By 7:20 a.m., the bus rolled out, and we reached school by 7:40 a.m. Classes started routinely, except we were ushered out of our old classrooms and into those of the seniors, reminding us we had some big shoes to fill. At 8:30 a.m., our juniors sauntered in, a glorious 30 minutes late. Watching them stroll in, we collectively thought, are these guys really made for this? But then again, we remembered we weren't much better last year.

During lunch, a few of us, led by the ever-curious Lahsun and Balli, decided to chat with the juniors. Before we knew it, the school grounds turned into a mini-reunion. Some of us decided to spice things up. Abhay was handed a special mission—talk to a girl and build some confidence. Simple, right? Well, Abhay had other plans. He didn't just strike up a conversation; he returned at the end of the break with crucial information from her: her Instagram ID.

But, of course, some *sanskari* soul (a teacher we still don't know) snitched to the director, and the blame landed squarely on Rana—who was napping in class the entire time!

◆◆◆

A few days before the juniors' grand arrival, the director decided to do a surprise check-in. Naturally, Rana, being Rana, was lounging in his usual dazed glory. The director, with his signature glare, asked, 'Rana, what exactly have you been doing these past few days?'

Rana, without a second of thought or an ounce of shame, grinned and said, 'Sir, I was… waiting for the juniors.' The room froze. Even Lahsun, who was mid-snack, choked on his biscuit. The director's face contorted somewhere between shock and the realisation that he was dealing with a lost cause.

Fast forward to the day of the juniors' first lunch break at school. Rana had apparently been dozing through class again, but this time, someone ratted us out for hanging around the juniors in the ground. The director swooped in like a hawk and went straight to Rana.

'What were you doing during lunch?' he barked.

Rana, desperately trying to appear studious, stammered, 'Sir, I was… uh, in the classroom… reading a book.'

The director's face turned tomato-red. 'If any of the Tigers step out of the Academy, I'll throw Rana out, too!'

For a moment, we all went silent. Even Lahsun whispered, 'Bro, I love my buddy; what if he actually gets kicked out?' But as soon as the director stormed off, the jokes started rolling. Balli patted Rana on the back. 'Don't worry, bro; we'll organise your farewell—full senior-style. Flowers, garlands, everything!'

The laughter, however, was short-lived. We soon discovered that Pomeranian's undy was homesick. Now, the stakes were higher. To keep Rana out of the spotlight, the drill instructors handed us a simple mission: protect Rana at all costs. We formed a covert team to shadow him everywhere. If he sneezed, we covered it up. If he fumbled, we blamed someone else.

One day in the mess, Rana absentmindedly knocked over a glass of milk. Without missing a beat, Lahsun exclaimed, 'Earthquake, guys! Everyone, hold your plates!' Rana's sheepish grin said it all, but we rallied behind him with laughter.

Hearing the word 'earthquake', I couldn't help but be reminded of our junior term's infamous late-night tremor. It was about 11:30 p.m., and I was sitting alone in my room, staring lazily at my almirah. Suddenly, it began to shake. My first thought—'Great, now I'm imagining things.' But then the entire room started swaying, and the dreaded hooter blared.

'EARTHQUAKE! EARTHQUAKE!' echoed down the corridors. Panic set in as cadets scrambled outside. I bolted down, too, still in my civil clothes. In the chaos, it didn't even cross my mind to grab my tracksuit. 'Who cares about dress codes when the ground itself is rebelling?' I thought. But there they were—our ever-dedicated seniors, unflinching and poised like gatekeepers of the protocol.

'Where are your tracksuits?' they demanded.

'Sir, the ground is literally shaking!' someone dared to retort.

'And your SHOES?'

'Sir, if the earth swallows us, no one's checking footwear,' I mumbled under my breath.

By the time the tremors stopped, half of us stood barefoot, a few wrapped in blankets, and one guy even clutched his pillow as though it might save him. Meanwhile, the seniors, perfectly dressed and standing tall, looked like they were ready for a photo-op instead of an emergency. When we arrived back in our rooms, we realised how Macchi had slept through the entire ordeal, unaware of the tremors beneath him. This became another story to tell in the course books.

In the end, nothing major happened. Rana was not kicked out (though we once did perform josh push-ups for his farewell), but the experience left us with a golden rule: never let Rana be the face of any operation.

◆◆◆

The long-anticipated day of the DST had finally arrived. The DST was no less than a battlefield—a test of precision, discipline, and nerves. Swaran Sahab, our drill instructor, had been eagerly waiting for this moment. 'DST *ka asli maza tabhi hai jab ek galti karte hi tumhe bahar nikaal diya jaye*,' he'd often say during practice.

The first day was the Alpha Squadron's turn, but here was the problem—none of us had a proper haircut. Even though we'd been sent on Liberty a few days back, we had collectively 'forgotten' to trim our hair. Rookie mistake.

As punishment, our test was pushed back, and the Charlie Squadron took our slot instead. Charlies, the golden boys of the Academy, walked into the test like they'd been born-ready. One cadet, who was the only untrimmed boy in the squadron, even trimmed his own hair—talk about dedication! Swaran Sahab saw him and immediately boomed, '*Yeh hota hai asli* soldier! Discipline *ka dusra naam*, Charlie Squadron!' He even smiled, which was so rare it felt like spotting a unicorn.

Of course, we knew the truth. It wasn't devotion—it was pure, unadulterated fear. Swaran Sahab's threats of ET weren't to be taken lightly. Because Alpha wasn't prepared for the DST and blatantly ignored the declared routine, the entire squadron faced Swaran Sahab's wrath. While other squadrons enjoyed their games period, we were ordered to do front rolls, push-ups, and *murga* walks across the field, all under the blazing sun.

'Alpha Squadron, you'll keep going until you sweat out all your excuses!' bellowed Swaran Sahab.

Meanwhile, Charlie was cheering over a goal, and Bravo was tossing their volleyball in the air while we Apaches turned the football field into a circus of misery. By the end, we weren't sure if we had improved discipline or just discovered new shades of regret.

Next up was the Bravo Squadron. Their test was slightly chaotic, with one guy forgetting the *tez chaal* timing and almost mowing down the director, but they somehow passed, with most of them making it through. The director, as always, started with a strict uniform inspection. Every element had to be flawless. Buttons? Exactly three visible, no more, no less. Belt? Aligned perfectly, not a millimetre out of place. Shoes? Polished to mirror-finish perfection. The tiniest mistake—a loose thread on a badge or a wrinkle in your shirt—was enough to get you booted out on the spot. And believe you me, it happened.

As the turn came for Alpha, we all felt a mix of excitement and anxiety. The previous squads had set the bar so high that we were determined not to let our squadron down. The uniform inspection passed smoothly—no one was thrown out, as we had all learned from the earlier stories of others who had faced the dreaded rejection. We had done our homework, ensuring everything was perfect down to the last button. When it came to the group drill, we nailed it! Our moves were sharp, our formations flawless—we were in sync like a well-oiled machine. The director nodded approvingly, but the real test was yet to come.

The individual performance was where the real challenge lay. One by one, each of us stepped up, and just as I thought I was doing well, boom! The director's voice cut through the air. 'Fail!' My heart sank. I couldn't believe it. Why me? The director gave a sharp look and said, 'Being a champion squadron is all well and good, but don't forget, drill squadrons also need their own finesse. Learn to balance both!' The words stung, but they lit a fire in me. I was determined to turn this around.

A few days passed, and the DST was scheduled once again. This time, I wasn't going to let anything slip. My buddy, the one who had become my unofficial drill coach, became my lifesaver. He dragged me into a room, where we practised endlessly. 'Come on, Shivam, you've got this! Just move like you're born to do it!' he'd encourage, even when my legs felt like they might fall off. There were times when I tripped over my own feet, but he would just laugh and say, 'No one's perfect—but we can at least be better than we were before!'

The day of the DST came, and I was ready. I felt the difference in my posture and the precision of my steps. I wasn't perfect, but I was so much better than the first time. As I executed the drill, I could feel the director's eyes on me. I was half-expecting the dreaded 'Fail!' to ring out again, but instead, a surprising remark came.

'Well, well, look at you. You've actually improved. Not perfect, but definitely a step up. Keep it up!'

My heart swelled with pride, and my buddy, who had been standing at the back, gave me a thumbs-up. The moment was sweet, but I knew this was just the beginning. I had gone from failing miserably to receiving praise for improvement—and that, I realised, was worth more than any perfect performance.

Making of the 'Bhaiii'

Apko pata hai PT ka aavishkar kisne kia tha!?
—PTI Ramkishan Sahab

Venturing into June, it started—the silence of Block 'B' marked the Academy becoming our own, with our juniors now gone for summer break. With them busy, we ruled the grounds. Of course, we never had the luxury of a summer break. Our batch had joined late in July, too late for a summer break, thanks to the delay in the tenth-grade exams. But this story isn't about our academic misfortunes; it's about hockey… or rather, my hockey adventures that cemented my legacy as 'Bhaiii' (with three 'I's, don't forget!).

The Academy had recently added hockey to the game curriculum. Being the jack of all trades (and master of none), I decided to give it a shot. I marched onto the field, confident as ever.

'*Arrey, Bhaiii!* Hockey *khelega*?' someone teased from the sidelines.

'*Kyu nahi*?' I replied, spinning the stick like a warrior preparing for battle.

First day, first practice. The ball was rolling toward me, and with all my might, I swung the stick. THWACK!

But no cheers followed. Instead, there was silence. Then, a low grunt. Turning my head, I saw Gulati, the gym freak, staring at his leg. A deep blue line was forming, courtesy of my 'precision'.

'*Bhaiii, yeh kya kiya?*' Gulati asked, barely holding back a smirk.

'*Arrey,* sorry *yaar, galti se lag gaya!*' I laughed nervously.

Fortunately, Gulati was built like a tank. He shrugged it off, muttering something about karma and beginners.

On the second day, I felt confident. After all, Gulati hadn't retaliated, and my 'training' seemed to be going well. That was until....

The ball was again coming my way. This time, my target wasn't the goal; it was the goat—the BCA of the Academy. He approached me, trying to snatch the ball.

'*Bhaiii,* ball pass *kar,*' he said with a sly grin.

'*Tu* ball *le ke toh dikha!*' I challenged him, adrenaline pumping.

And then, I swung. The ball missed him entirely, but my stick... didn't. THWACK! Right on his leg.

'Bhaaaaiiii,' he roared, dropping to the ground like a goat caught in headlights.

The field erupted in laughter. I, too, couldn't help but laugh, though guilt began creeping in. The BCA limped off, muttering something about revenge while the others teased me relentlessly.

'*Bhaiii,* hockey *ka Jaadugar*!' someone shouted.

By now, my reputation was set. But I wasn't ready to give up. *Teesri baar toh* lucky *hota hai na*?

Enter Chawal. He was the most agile player on the field, darting around like a pro. Determined to prove myself, I charged forward as he dribbled past me.

'Bro, *aa raha hoon!* Ready *ho ja,*' I shouted.

'*Tu bas dekh,*' Chawal replied, smirking.

The ball rolled in my direction. I raised my stick, and... THWACK!

But this time, too, it wasn't the ball. Chawal stopped in his tracks, his leg bearing the brunt of my over-enthusiasm. He let out a yelp and fell to the ground. The injury was serious enough to send him to the hospital. For five days, he walked like Pushpa—the iconic strut from the movie that had just been released.

'*Arrey Bhaiii,* hockey *chod de!* Academy *ko baksh de*!' someone joked as I tried to hide my face in shame.

From that day, my legacy was sealed. Everywhere I went, people shouted '*Bhaiii!*' It wasn't just a nickname; it was a reminder of my 'illustrious' hockey career.

The moment I left the dream of hockey behind, I dove straight into swimming. In June, swimming was the best way to stay calm, cool, and composed. It felt like a mini-vacation every time we dived into that pool. The funny part was that Rajinder Sahab rarely interfered. It was like we were given free rein to do whatever we wanted in the water—swimming, splashing and catching each other like kids in a water park.

But then, of course, when things got out of hand, Rajinder Sahab would pop up like a lifeguard on a mission. 'Alright, you troublemakers, 100 m, now!' he'd announce, and we had to swim four continuous laps. No one ever dared to deny him, and let me tell you, those 100 m races were like a test of survival.

But in the end, swimming was the only way to survive summer. Without it, we'd have melted into puddles.

Now, after every swim, there was the dressing-up drama. Some of the warriors would take ages to get into their games gear. I swear, it was like watching a sloth trying to put on clothes. And what would our PT instructor do? Oh, he'd make them do frog jumps or roll across the changing room floor, from the locker to the fall-in spot, just to speed them up. 'Come on, hop, hop! It's not a fashion show!' he'd shout, and those poor guys were hopping like frogs in front of everyone.

◆◆◆

It was the time when school classes were about to shift entirely to the Academy campus, and, let me tell you, life suddenly turned into a military drill... quite literally. With the juniors on break, the instructors would often sneak around, turning us into their live entertainment show. The teachers, too, had to come all the way to the Academy to teach us, as our half-yearly exams were planned within those hallowed walls.

Now, here's where things got serious. The director himself was hovering around, and to make it worse, the drill instructor made his legendary rounds every fifteen minutes. Nobody dared to sleep or even blink for too long, lest you risk becoming his next target. 'You think this is a resort? Stand up! Front roll to the gate and back!' he'd bark. I swear, even the toughest among us sat straighter than a ruler.

Classes were held in Lecture Halls 3 and 4, which, being on the upper floor, felt like giant microwaves on full blast. Both coolers roared like jet engines, but they did little to stop the sweat from dripping like a leaky tap. And God forbid the teacher was late! The entire gang would huddle in Lecture Hall 3, peeking out of the windows like spies on a mission, scanning the parking lot for any sign of movement. 'Is that someone in a *saari*? No? False alarm!' someone would whisper, and we'd all dive back into our seats like it was a game of musical chairs.

The real fun began when we spotted the 'H' Section's English teacher walking in. Oh, she was a gem—every section's favourite because of her charming habit of forgetting all our names. 'You... uh... Shivendra? No? Shyam? Whatever, you at the back, stop talking!' she'd say, leaving the whole class stifling laughter. She was so lenient that even the most notorious pranksters could nap through her lectures. Honestly, she was more of a blessing than a teacher.

But then there was the 'S' Section's English teacher, a completely different species. This teacher didn't just command respect; she demanded it with a glare so powerful it could silence a hurricane. She had a knack for spotting sleepers from miles away. 'Yes, you, with your head bobbing like a dashboard toy, stand up and recite Lancho's soliloquy—NOW!' she'd say, and you could almost see the poor guy's soul leave his body.

'Ma'am, uh, I don't remember—'

'Oh, don't worry. You'll remember by the end of the day. Shall I call the drill instructor for some "memory improvement" exercises?' she'd reply with a sly grin.

Her ability to maintain absolute control over the class was unmatched. Even the jokers would shrink under her gaze, their jokes dying in their throats.

Meanwhile, back in Lecture Hall 3, during one of those classic 'teacher late' moments, someone decided it was a good idea to mimic the drill instructor. '*Aye*, cadet! Why are you sitting like you're on a honeymoon?' one guy shouted, mimicking his tone perfectly. Everyone burst out laughing, but then the real drill instructor appeared out of nowhere. The silence that followed could have made even a graveyard seem lively.

Achievers' Day

Gentlemen, you are the 'Cream of Punjab'!

Excitement filled the air as Achievers' Day, the day that every AFPI cadet dreams of, finally arrived, and man, it felt like the entire Academy was vibrating with energy. This was the day when the newly commissioned officers flaunted their uniforms, and we, the ones still under training, got to join them in celebrating their hard-earned success. It was like a mini-reunion of sorts, where those who made it to NDA, OTA (Officers Training Academy), IMA (Indian Military Academy), and every other training Academy came together to share their war stories and wisdom.

You could feel the pride in the air—the newly commissioned officers were walking with a swagger, and rightly so. They had been through it all. As we gathered around them, I swear it felt like we were meeting legends. They had conquered the toughest training and earned their stripes, and now, it was their turn to shine.

The highlight of the day was when the director himself honoured them with the Maharaja Ranjit Singh Trophy, the most iconic trophy that made all of us feel like it was within our reach… someday.

Holding that trophy? It's like a dream come true for every AFPI cadet. It's not just a shiny piece of wood; it's the symbol of everything you've fought for—your sweat, your tears, and the endless hours of struggle. You could see the pride in the faces of those officers.

The officers shared their personal stories from their Academy days. We asked, 'Sir, are the punishments like what we get here at AFPI?' One officer, with a devilish grin, replied, 'Oh, you're getting prepared for something much bigger, trust me.' And then, he launched into a story that made us all feel thankful for every single push-up we'd ever done.

He told us about one of his mates who had failed a subject at the Academy and decided to 'help himself' by shifting his grades from 1.5 to 17.5—just to pass. But, as you can imagine, the teacher noticed something was off when an extra student passed with flying colours. The teacher immediately reported it to the adjutant of the Academy, and that's when the real punishment began.

The adjutant didn't waste any time. He called in the sixth-term cadets and gave them a two-hour lecture about the importance of leading by example, with punishment, too. But the real fun came after. 'You guys teach your juniors this?' The sixth-termers were sent to the field, and they punished the first-termers from 4:00 p.m. on Friday until 6:00 a.m. on Monday. Talk about a weekend getaway, right? Except it was the worst kind of weekend getaway.

As if that wasn't enough, the officer continued, 'On top of that, we had to run cross-country—5 km straight—then we had front rolls for another five.'

But it didn't stop there. The officer then told us about an incident with one of his friends. 'Panda, I think you're going to appreciate this one,' he said. Apparently, during that infamous cross-country run, they had to take off their shoes and climb a rope. Well, one cadet's foot got injured in the process, and when he tried to put his shoe back on, it became infected, causing his foot to swell up like a balloon. So, what happened next? 'They had to cut off his shoe to get it off, and he was immediately sent to the Military Hospital (MH) for a 14-day rest.'

The MH was the place every cadet dreamt of, not because of the medical care but because it's the only place where you get a break. No drills, no PT—just relaxation and a chance to recover. When we heard about sending him to the MH for his foot injury, he looked like he had just won the lottery. 'You wouldn't believe how relaxing it was,' he said with a grin. 'Fourteen days of just chilling out; it was like a vacation!'

We all laughed, but we also knew it was a punishment we never wanted to experience. The MH might have sounded like paradise, but it came at a price.

But something like this did happen at AFPI, too.

At the Academy, falling sick is rare—it's like the Academy builds your immune system out of steel. Colds, fevers? Forget it. But here's the thing: if you ever do feel like wanting to visit the hospital, you need to show it on paper. And why wouldn't you? That place isn't a hospital—it's a five-star hotel disguised as a medical facility.

The moment you step through those gates, it's like you've entered another world. All kinds of cuisines await you on the top floor, from butter chicken to biryani, with desserts that could make a cadet weep tears of joy. There's even a side hustle by nearby shops, ready to deliver chocolates, chips, and everything your Academy diet restricts. Some cadets would even schedule haircuts there—not because they cared about their hair—but because avoiding the Academy barber's 'military-grade scalping' was a luxury worth risking it all for.

So, the hospital was more than just a medical facility. It was freedom—freedom to eat, to skip games periods, and, for a few glorious hours, to not feel like you are part of a boot camp.

Now, let me tell you about the incident. One fine day, Tatyaal and Malhi came up with a genius plan to take a 'strategic withdrawal' from the Academy routine. Their destination? The hospital, of course.

The two reached the top floor, dreaming of the treasures that awaited them. The holy grail: butter naan and a steaming plate of momos. They had barely started their feast when the unthinkable happened: Atma Sahab walked in. Yes, Atma Sahab—the human radar. He had somehow sensed their treachery and tracked them down faster than a missile lock.

You should've seen their faces: Malhi froze mid-bite, his samosa dripping chutney onto the floor. Tatyaal? He tried to blend in with the curtains, which, I would say, didn't work.

Atma Sahab didn't even have to say anything; his glare did all the talking. 'Back to the Academy. NOW.' Their dreams of a quiet, indulgent escape were dashed. But, of course, there was one cadet who thought he could negotiate. Legend has it that Tatyaal tried to argue about the 'digestive benefits' of hospital food over Academy meals. Needless to say, it didn't end well.

If you're curious about the aftermath, just ask Swaran Sahab. He'll tell you all about how Tatyaal and Malhi spent the next week doing 'voluntary' extra drills. The moral of the story? The hospital might be heaven, but Atma Sahab is the gatekeeper—and no one sneaks past him.

◆◆◆

But what if you were actually sick? At AFPI, where survival is the real curriculum, I—the strongest Apache junior (sarcasm fully intended)—was about to prove just how 'strong' I really was. With my unbeatable combination of clearing BPT and being a 'decent' runner, I thought I was invincible. Oh, how wrong I was.

The night before, a fever hit me harder than Swaran Sahab's punishments. But instead of doing the sensible thing, I skipped dinner and took medicine on an empty stomach. Because, obviously, I wanted to test if my stomach could multitask. Morning rolled around, and I dragged myself to the prayer lineup, barely holding on to reality.

Baghdadi started the prayer, his voice booming: 'Dear God, we pray to thee…' and trust me, it felt like 'thee' was summoning me directly. My vision blurred, my legs wobbled, and I grabbed KG's hand for dear life. KG, being the absolute gem that he was, muttered, 'Stop acting, bro,' and swatted me off like I was an annoying fly.

Seconds later, my legs gave up on me entirely, and I dropped. Straight. Like. A. Stick. Dada, ever the vigilant warrior, thought I was launching some kind of attack and sidestepped me with military precision. I collapsed in perfect parade position, stiff and dramatic, while chaos erupted around me.

Now, here's the kicker: the prayer didn't stop. Rajinder Sahab, in full discipline mode, didn't even blink. The man stood there like a statue, silently judging the collapse of my entire existence. It wasn't until KG finally realised that I wasn't joking that he grabbed me and dragged me to my room, with Swaran Sahab following behind to check if I was still alive.

But oh no, the drama didn't end there. Enter Warden Sahab, who stormed into my room like I'd committed a national crime by falling sick. 'You're taking weight-loss medicine, aren't you?!' he bellowed as if I'd smuggled contraband into the barracks. I blinked at him, genuinely confused. 'Sir, I'm already 10% of a human! Why would I want to disappear completely?' I protested, but Warden Sahab wasn't having it. He left with a huff, leaving me to wonder how fainting turned into a pharmaceutical conspiracy.

Just when I thought it was over, Atma Sahab appeared, looking calm and collected. 'You okay, cadet?' he asked, giving me the only moment of sanity in this circus. After confirming I was alive, he left to attend the fall-in lineup. From my room, I could hear the punishment unfolding—push-ups for everyone, all in my honour, while I lay there, listening to the chaos like it was my personal theme music.

The moral of this story? At AFPI, even passing out turns into a team-building exercise. And no, I'm not taking weight-loss medicine, but thanks for the concern, Warden Sahab.

◆◆◆

Back to the Achievers', after all the stories and motivation, we were in all-time high excitement. The achievers of the day were all set to celebrate in their own way, booking places we couldn't even dream of entering because of our under-eighteen status. But, of course, we weren't going to sit back and sulk. Oh no, we had our own grand plans.

As the day was winding down and the seniors started to head off, we knew there was one more big moment left: the party. With a twinkle in our eyes and a lot of enthusiasm, we approached the newly commissioned officers. 'Kushal, sir, about that party...?' And within seconds, we had the money in our hands! You would think we had just won the lottery. But no, it was our ticket to one of the most legendary evenings of our Academy life.

The director, ever the generous soul, declared that we would have Liberty from four to nine in the evening, the first time we were granted such a Liberty.

As usual, Tatyaal, our self-proclaimed 'finance minister', took charge. '*Sab paisa mere paas,*' he declared.

Tatyaal pulled out his phone. '*Bhai log, paanch* cabs book *karunga.*'

Each cab was packed with five-six people, resembling an overcrowded auto on a Delhi street. As the engines roared, it felt like Formula 1 was happening on the narrow roads of our town. The moment we hit the road, chaos ensued.

In the first cab:

Sosa: '*Oye* driver Sahab, *wo saamne wali* cab *dekh rahe ho? Uska* driver *so raha hai! Usko* overtake *karo, aaj ka khana meri taraf se!*'

Driver: '*Beta, mera* license *mat* cancel *karwa dena.* Race *toh main ladunga, lekin thoda zyada mat bolna.*'

In the second cab:

Mushki (sticking his head out of the window): '*Bhaiyo, dekh lo! Yeh chehra yaad rakhna, hum* champion *hai!*'

Bakra: 'Champion? *Teri shakal dekh ke toh* driver *apna* metre reverse *karega!*'

Driver (laughing): '*Aap log* race *karne aaye ho ya* comedy *karne?*'

In the third cab:

Lahsun: 'Driver Sahab, *peechhe wali* cab *mein mere dushman baithe hain. Ek baar unko* overtake *karwa do, taaki zindagi bhar unko yaad rahe ki baap kaun hai!*'

Driver: '*Arre bhai, main* driver *hoon ya supari* killer?'

Gyani: '*Arre* seatbelt *se kya hoga? Agar hum* crash *karenge toh* news *mein* headline *toh* "junior F1 racers" *banegi!*'

The real drama started when the cabs came close to each other. Bakra and Balli started making faces at Mushki from their window, sticking out their tongues and pointing fingers. Mushki, being Mushki, yelled back, '*Oye, dhyan se! Tumhari gaadi mein Tatyaal hai, agar paisa gir gaya toh* driver *bhi bhaag jayega!*'

One cab sped past the others, its passengers screaming, 'Sir, pass *karo!* Sir, pass *karo! Aaj hum* first reach *karenge, baaki sab* second-hand *hai!*'

In retaliation, another cab driver yelled, '*Arre unki gaadi mein* petrol *kam hai, chinta mat karo!*'

Meanwhile, Kansal, sitting in one of the back cabs, looked worried. '*Bhai, yeh sab toh theek hai, par Tayaal paisa leke bhaag na jaye!*'

Dada: '*Arre* tension *mat le, woh bhag gaya toh* PTI *ki ek* kick *kaafi hai uske* future *ke liye.*'

Finally, we all reached the destination—not before two cabs missed the turn and had to take a U-turn that cost them their pole position. The drivers parked, exchanged looks of exhaustion, and muttered something about 'life insurance' under their breath.

Standing together, out of breath and laughing, Gyani declared, '*Aaj ka* lesson simple *hai, bhaiyo. Tatyaal ko* finance minister *banana nuksaan hai, aur* Formula 1 *ka sapna humein chod dena chahiye.*'

As we entered the venue, with faces red from all the yelling and laughing, we realised that the night had just begun. Who needed fancy clubs when Liberty itself was this adventurous?

The theatre was ours. Yes, you heard that right—booked entirely by us. Tatyaal, our 'financial genius', had redeemed himself after Gyani's snarky comment. It was one of those rare moments when you looked around and felt like royalty. The rows of chairs were fully occupied by men in mufti, each looking as if they owned the world. Forget the boring movie playing on the screen; this was our time to shine.

As the lights dimmed and the screen lit up, Sosa, in his usual theatrical tone, said, '*Bhaiyon, ek shaandar raat ki shuruat ho chuki hai! Lekin* movie *ke baare mein zyada umeed mat rakhna.*'

Lahsun, who had already scanned the entire theatre for potential 'beauty spots', muttered, '*Bhai,* movie *chhodo, dikhe koi kaalein milein toh batao.*'

To mark the moment, Kansal suggested we click a group picture. With the precision of a military drill, we lined up strategically, making sure to capture every single chair in the frame. The result? A panoramic masterpiece of camaraderie, with Gyani standing front and centre, hands spread like Shahrukh Khan, proclaiming, '*Yeh sab hamara hai!*'

The movie started, but calling it boring would be an understatement. Even a government seminar on waste management would've been more entertaining.

As popcorn and cokes arrived, the true entertainment began.

Balli, who could never eat quietly, started crunching loudly. '*Abe Balli, tu* popcorn *kha raha hai ya patakhe phod raha hai?*' teased Bagdadi.

Sariya added, '*Aur dekh,* cola *ke saath* popcorn *nahi, pani piyo.* Healthy *raho,* fit *raho!*'

Every so often, someone would whisper about their 'crush' or speculate on what snacks the achievers were having at their grand party.

By the time the movie ended (or, let's say, people woke up), the idea of snacks sounded more exciting than ever. We headed to the food court.

As the clock struck eight-fifty, the time caught up with us. '*Bhai,* Academy *waapas jana hai!*' said Lahsun. The scramble for cabs began. Many resorted to autos, the undisputed king of Indian overloading. We stuffed ourselves in like a wedding buffet plate—six jammed into the middle section like sardines, two clinging to the front like co-pilots of a spaceship, three somehow wedged into the tiny backspace, and one ultimate survivor sprawled across the mess of legs like a defeated wrestler.

At the Academy gate, Warden Sahab was waiting like Yamraj, arms crossed.

'*Nau baj gaye. Kahan the tum log? Tum log samajhte ho ki* Liberty picnic *hai?* Next time late *hue toh* Liberty cancel!'

As we walked back to our barracks, someone whispered, 'Liberty cancel *toh hoti nahi, par suna dete hain.*'

That night, as we lay in our bunks, we knew we had created memories for a lifetime. Because the movie may have been forgettable, but the laughter, the brotherhood, and the drama? Absolutely unforgettable. No training, no drills, just good food and good company. I swear, it felt like a dream. Whoever thought of this idea is a genius (though the person who chose the movie deserves a separate punishment).

Marry-Go-Round

Beta, time to bura hi chal rha hai!
—Sunil Sir, Shemrock

Yesterday's lessons felt like a distant memory as the school classes were coming to an end, and the dreaded half-yearly exams loomed like storm clouds over our heads. Teachers would march into the Academy halls daily, their arms full of papers, like soldiers gearing up for battle. Cheating? Out of the question. Not because we were noble but because the cameras and the staff had eyes sharper than a hawk.

It was the English exam—a subject no one dared cheat in. But trust Tatyaal to break the mould. All he wanted was to confirm the letter-writing format, just a harmless peek. Enter Ms Birinder. She swooped in like a hawk spotting a prey, cancelling his paper with the efficiency of a firing squad.

'Ma'am,' pleaded Tatyaal, 'I swear I wasn't cheating. I was just... double-checking!'

Ms Birinder wasn't buying it. The report zoomed straight to the director. 'What do you want me to do with him?' she asked. 'Cancel his exam if you think he deserves it,' came the director's reply. 'After all, it's your subject.'

And yet, Tatyaal—our legend—managed to score 74% overall, even with a fat zero in English. Truly, the stuff of academic legends.

Now, exams brought their own brand of misery, but nothing compared to PT during exam season. It was mandatory, even on the day before exams. As if the stress of studies wasn't enough, we had to sweat it out on the ground, too. But then came my birthday—my 'special' day.

I wasn't about to let it become an open invitation for birthday bumps. So, I teamed up with DST and Doda for the ultimate survival plan: Operation Hide Shivam.

'Bro,' said DST, 'I'll empty my almirah. You can hide there. It's foolproof!'

'Foolproof?' I snorted. 'Or Shivam-proof?'

He shoved the last of his belongings into a corner, creating just enough space for me to squeeze in. By 11:50 p.m., I was locked inside. Outside, the predators prowled.

'Where is he?' barked Sariya.

'Probably hiding under his bed,' someone suggested. They ransacked the room with the enthusiasm of treasure hunters but found nothing. Furious, they decided to exact their revenge on my room. Buckets of water were flung with the precision of Olympic athletes. My room was transformed into an aquatic theme park.

At 1:30 a.m., I finally emerged from my almirah sanctuary, only to find my room resembling a swimming pool. 'Happy Birthday, *Bhaiii*,' Doda chuckled as I tiptoed to bed, avoiding the puddles. The next morning, with soggy shoes and a sleep-deprived brain, I sat for my exam.

By evening, the celebrations were in full swing at Tehla Mall. A grand party, laughter, and endless jokes marked the end of exams and the beginning of our two-day home break.

Those 48 hours at home were a whirlwind—movies, calls, and endless discussions. By the time we returned, we knew the grind awaited: NDA classes, PT, games, and all the chaos of Academy life.

◆◆◆

The day we arrived at the Academy, the air was filled with excitement and nervous energy. Cadets were greeting each other, giving high fives, slapping backs, and just generally causing chaos. But amidst all that, we knew something special was lurking—the written examination! The tension was palpable, but at least we could take comfort in the fact that it wasn't going to be all work and no play.

The first day was definitely different. We woke up early for PT, our muscles screaming in protest, but now the real challenge began: sleep was going to be a rare commodity. We had to be ready for classes by 8 a.m. But, oh, what a myth that was—the real myth was the idea that we'd actually be able to sleep in.

Our timetable? A roller coaster ride. First up, Physics and Chemistry alternated in the mornings—a mental workout that left us wondering if we'd have time to even breathe. Next came English and GK (General Knowledge), and oh, let me tell you about the English classes.

Bahuguna Sir, the legendary CO, was the one who taught us English, and believe me when I say he was a master at keeping us on our toes. He knew exactly how to crack jokes when we were too serious and how to bring us back to earth when we were too casual. The moment he entered the class, it was like the room came alive. He looked at us, grinning like he knew a secret, and dropped the line that made us all chuckle:

'Gentlemen, you are the "Cream of Punjab". But I want that cream to turn into butter! So, give me your best and let's churn out the best cadets possible!'

That line became legendary. I remember calling my parents later that day and telling them about it. Just for fun, they responded, 'Don't worry, *beta*, you're that milk that comes out when you're trying to pick up the cream for ghee!' For a second, I was like, did my parents just roast me?! But I couldn't help laughing. They were like my personal comedy show on the phone!

Bahuguna Sir was a master of making even the most stressful situations light-hearted. 'Gentlemen, don't take tension. The written exam is easy—just be attentive.'

Then came our Maths classes—with Raj Sir. Now, Raj Sir was a whole different level of character. His idea of teaching? No filter, just straight-up blunt statements that would hit you like a ton of bricks. One moment, he'd say something so out-of-pocket, you'd think, 'Did I just hear that correctly?'

I remember this one time Raj Sir was explaining a complex Maths formula when he turned to one of us and said, 'If you're going to fail, at least fail with style, okay?' That was it. We were all left laughing for a good ten minutes, but when it was time to work, he was serious. Real serious.

After that came lunch, and oh, the first time we saw the juniors arriving was... an eye-opener. We thought, 'Man, their life must be so easy right now.' But soon, we realised that they were going to taste what we were experiencing all too soon.

Then, of course, came 'break time', or as I liked to call it, the not-really-a-break time. We had assignments to do, Mathematics questions to solve, and endless revisions for exams. During what was supposed to be our 'break', we found ourselves buried in homework. Who knew that a break would feel more like a marathon?

The real gem, though, was our English class. I swear, it felt like we were all getting a fresh start every time we walked into that class. Bahuguna Sir had this amazing ability to make the toughest lessons feel like we were just chatting. I remember one day, he took us out to the field, divided us into teams, and set up questions to be answered. Whoever lost had to do 50 push-ups. At that moment, it wasn't about the answers anymore—it was about winning. The competition was on, and we were all in it to win it.

And then came the half-yearly results. The atmosphere in the room was tense. The names of cadets who scored above 85% were announced, and finally, Singla, who had missed the torch[1] twice, earned his torch! A lot of cadets had missed the mark, and some even had their torches taken away, like DST, Rishi, and our beloved SCC.

1 A 'torch' is an academic honor worn on the uniform, similar to army medals, awarded to cadets scoring above a certain percentage.

That moment was rough. You could see the disappointment on their faces. But soon enough, we learned the most valuable lesson—there's always a silver lining. The cadets who missed out on their torches were given a chance to earn them back, which gave us an excuse to throw another party.

◆◆◆

A few days later, it was one of those sweltering July nights when even the walls of AFPI seemed to sweat. The fans spun uselessly, barely stirring the suffocating air, and the power had decided to abandon us entirely. In true Alpha Block fashion, the seniors found a way to turn the misery into mayhem. Old Kishore Kumar hits echoed down the corridors, sung with a mix of genuine nostalgia and spectacularly off-key enthusiasm. From somewhere in the darkness, exaggerated moans of despair added an oddly artistic touch to the soundtrack of the night. It was chaos—but the kind that felt like home, a mess we'd remember forever.

But that night, our juniors decided to make it unforgettable—and not in a good way.

Around midnight, as our voices reached their peak, we noticed something peculiar. A beam of light was flickering from the direction of the junior block. At first, we ignored it, thinking someone was just fooling around with a torch. But soon, the flickers turned into a full-on light show.

And then, the unthinkable happened. About 15–20 juniors emerged in a room, forming what can only be described as a 'dance troupe'. With torchlights acting as their spotlights, they danced their hearts out. From Nora Fatehi's sultry moves to Jacqueline Fernandez's Bollywood swag, they were recreating everything—and that too with their backs towards us like they were saying, 'Hips don't lie!'

Guruji, our beloved mimic, whispered, 'From our knock knock to their *nach baliye, yeh* juniors *toh naye rang dikhane lage!*' That comment was enough to send us into muffled fits of laughter.

Their dance was chaotic yet entertaining. Two juniors acted as the light operators, making sure the 'stage' was well lit. Their moves?

Well, they made our childhood school performances look like Broadway productions. But the cherry on top? One junior attempted a backflip and landed straight on his back with a loud 'Thud!' Even the dancers paused for a second before continuing their 'show'.

By now, we couldn't hold it in. '*Yeh toh hadd hai*!' whispered Bagdadi, wiping tears of laughter. But as much as we enjoyed the show, it was a breach of discipline, and we knew it was time to act.

Some appointments went to inform the guard. Within minutes, a small squad marched to the junior block. The moment they reached, the scene flipped like a movie climax. The music stopped, torches disappeared, and the juniors scattered like cockroaches when the guard and appointments approached that block.

But alas, one poor soul didn't make it. When the guard banged on his door, the junior, still half-asleep, yelled in true Jethalal style, '*Kaun hai be!?*'

From outside, the guard bellowed, '*Tera Baap*!' The mix of panic and confusion on the junior's face was priceless.

The next morning, a Sunday, was declared 'Tiger Training Day'. Groups of juniors were lined up under the command of appointments. Push-ups, squats, handstands—you name it, they did it. One particularly enthusiastic appointment, the senior sergeant, made a junior practice saluting fifty times.

Even amidst all this, there was no hostility—just a strict reminder of discipline. After all, we had been in their shoes last year. As the Tigers were sweating it out, Guruji joked when we entered to see my understudy, 'Nora Fatehi *ko dekhne aaye the, aur yahan* PT *ho rahi hai!*'.

That night, back in Alpha Block, the power cut persisted. With no fans and no respite from the July heat, we decided to improvise. Everyone dragged their mattresses to the top floor corridor, where the windows provided a faint breeze. It became a makeshift dormitory.

Around twenty of us lined up like sardines in a can. Some were in proper night suits, while others, embracing the heat, stuck to their undergarments. The windows were wide open, letting in occasional gusts of warm air and the distant hum of crickets.

Sleep was a challenge. Kansal, always the innovator, suggested using wet towels as cooling blankets. It worked—for five minutes—until someone accidentally flung theirs onto another cadet's face.

By morning, the scene was pure chaos. Legs were dangling over shoulders, some cadets had rotated from vertical to horizontal, and one poor guy was clutching someone else's pillow like it was his long-lost teddy bear. I couldn't help but burst out laughing when I saw Gyani sleeping diagonally, one leg stretched onto Sosa's chest, who, in turn, was mumbling something about 'crushes' in his sleep.

Balli, the early riser, looked around and exclaimed, '*Bhai, yeh hai kya,* wake them up. If the warden found us like this, for sure, we are off going for punishment?'

It was one of those nights that reminded us that while discipline and respect were paramount, it was these quirky, funny moments that truly bonded us as brothers. AFPI wasn't just an Academy; it was home, where even torchlight dances and overcrowded mattresses became cherished memories.

A few days after that incident, my coursemate Rishi hit me with the kind of news that could only come from him. He casually dropped, 'Bro, your understudy scored 98% in class Tenth, and you were at 94%! What's up with that?' I thought he was messing with me. I mean, who scores 98%? Was this guy secretly a robot or something? But nope, Rishi wasn't kidding. 98%—he really said it like it was a casual Tuesday.

Then, later that day, my undy, Param, came bouncing up to me, grinning as if he'd just won the lottery. 'Sir, I got Alpha Sergeant!' he announced. I didn't even crack a smile. On the inside, though, I was dying of laughter. All I could think was, 'Well, here we go—this is gonna be fun.' There he was, blissfully unaware, thinking he'd just entered the VIP section. Little did he know, he had just joined the 'Appointment Pain Club'.

I had to hold back my laughter, though, because the real comedy hadn't even begun. Sure, he got Alpha Sergeant, but with that came a delightful new world of responsibility. And by responsibility, I mean getting blamed for everything under the sun. Every time one of the

Alpha Tigers messed up, guess who was going to get roasted by the staff and also by us? Guess who was going to be the human punching bag for every tiny mistake? My poor, naïve understudy.

So, instead of bursting his bubble, I thought, 'Let him ride the wave of glory. The fall will be so much sweeter when it comes.' He thought he was walking into a parade, but little did he know that the parade was just a setup for the most spectacular crash landing. I might not have smiled, but in my head, I was rolling on the floor laughing. Time to watch him learn the real meaning of appointment—duties later, punishments first!

Entropy & Enthalpy

Phas mat jana!!
—Warden Sahab

Operation Night Out, the infamous event, was a legendary tale passed down through generations at the Academy, a rite of passage for the brave and the foolish alike. The legacy began with our seniors and their daring escapades through the bathroom window. When every other window was sealed tighter than a submarine hatch, this lone bathroom window, tucked away in a forgotten corner, became the last bastion of hope for cadets seeking freedom under the cover of darkness.

One fateful night, the torch of this daring tradition was picked up by Lahsun, Mau, and Moan. Fuelled by their thirst for adventure (and possibly boredom), they hatched their plan. It wasn't just a stroll in the moonlight; no, this was a full-fledged military operation.

The Plan: The bathroom window, strategically located in Panda's room, served as the point of exit. The target was simple—get out, enjoy the night, and get back without alerting the hawk-eyed guards or the cameras.

The operation began with Mau, the designated scout, peeking out to ensure that the coast was clear. Lahsun, true to his name, spread the word (and himself) everywhere, prepping the team for the mission. Finally, Moan, the techie, devised the escape route, complete with a detailed map and plans drawn on a napkin he 'borrowed' from the mess.

They crept through the dorms like commandos, their breath barely audible, their eyes scanning for the patrolling guards. The guards' movement was unpredictable, like drunken sloths on caffeine. Every cadet knew the drill: If spotted, vanish like a ghost.

The Execution: The trio slipped out through the bathroom window like shadows, each one holding their breath as they dropped down into the cold, wet grass below. They sprinted to the boundary wall, pausing only to check for guards. Once clear, Moan provided a boost, and one by one, they scaled the wall like nimble monkeys.

Once outside, their adventure began—only to realise they had forgotten one crucial detail: money. With their pockets emptier than their stomachs after a PT session, they called in reinforcements. Enter PT and Husn, the cavalry. The duo brought supplies (read: pocket change) and joined the operation, making it a five-man squad.

The night was perfect—or so they thought.

Unbeknownst to them, the Academy's infamous cameras had captured every move. The next morning, in the fall-in parade, the news hit like an artillery shell.

'Five cadets caught on camera during a night out and the sixth, the room owner!'

What followed was a spectacle. The director, livid and legendary for his temper, declared, '21 ETs each!' For the uninitiated, that meant 21 punishment days designed to break your soul and your body.

On the tracks, under the blazing sun, Swaran Sahab took over. This man was not a trainer; he was a tormentor sent from another dimension. 'ROLL! Don't crawl, ROLL!' he barked as the culprits rolled like rotisserie chickens on the tracks, their dignity left behind at the wall they had so heroically scaled the previous night.

Meanwhile… the rest of us, who had nothing to do with the escapade, turned the punishment into a spectator sport. While they rolled, we cheered, gambled on who would puke first, and even created a makeshift 'penalty board'. Lahsun resembled a garlic clove rolling in mud, while Mau looked like he was auditioning for a circus act. As for Moan, his moans were louder than the orders being shouted at him.

The ordeals didn't stop there. Between push-ups, frog jumps, and bear crawls, they had to scream, 'I AM A FOOL FOR GETTING CAUGHT!' at the top of their lungs. This went on for hours, punctuated by Swaran Sahab's threats of 'extra ETs if I hear any whining!'

That night, the rest of us celebrated their bravery (and stupidity) by re-enacting their operation in our dorms, complete with sound effects. Panda, whose bathroom window had been the infamous exit, claimed that he had no idea. 'I was asleep!' he protested, though we all knew he was silently laughing inside.

Lessons Learned:

1. Always carry money.
2. Never underestimate the Academy's surveillance system.
3. If you're going to get caught, make sure it's worth the punishment.

To this day, Operation Night Out remains a cautionary tale and a source of endless laughter. The bathroom window? Sealed shut the very next day. But like they say in the Academy: When one window closes, another opens… if you're brave enough to find it.

◆◆◆

While we were stuck in this hell of a routine, our juniors at school were having a whole different story going on. It was a regular day at school, and everything was going smoothly until our Chemistry class was interrupted by chaos. Out of nowhere, a panicked cry erupted: 'Chuha! Chuha! Monty!' At that very moment, everyone knew what the commotion was about. Let me introduce you to a permanent resident of AFPI—'Monty', the most fearless and oversized mouse you'd ever see. Bigger than a kitten, Monty wasn't just any mouse; he was a legend.

Monty had a reputation. On the ground floor, his appearances were common, and on the first floor, he'd occasionally roam around. But if you spotted him on the top floor, you knew Monty was on some kind of caffeine overdose. That day, though, Monty outdid himself. The commotion started in the junior batch when Nirbhik, one of our juniors, decided to casually open his bag. And out sprang Monty, like a star performer making a grand entrance!

For a moment, his classmates thought it was a prank. '*Kya bakwas kar raha hai,* Nirbhik?!' But when the teacher caught sight of Monty, all doubts were cleared. The classroom erupted in chaos. The teacher, caught between bravery and instinct, opened the door wide and yelled, '*Ise bahar nikaalo!*' But Monty had other plans. It did leave the classroom at its own will, only to run into Seema Ma'am's—our coordinator's—office.

The juniors, caught in the frenzy, ran after Monty, yelling, 'Ma'am, please don't call anyone. *Ye* AFPI *ka chuha hai! Sirf hum nikaalenge!*' Their reasoning? Well, Monty wasn't your regular mouse; he was practically a cadet. 'School staff cannot touch him,' they declared with pride. 'Civilian *chuha toh uska saamna bhi nahi kar sakta! Ye toh* push-ups *bhi hamare saath karta hai!*'

When Seema Ma'am heard that Monty did push-ups with the cadets, she didn't know whether to laugh or cry. And as the juniors desperately tried to lure Monty out of her office, Monty decided to flex his agility. He jumped onto her almirah, ran across her desk, and finally squeezed through a tiny opening near the door. Chaos temporarily ended.

Later, when Brinder Ma'am narrated the whole episode to us seniors in the middle of class, we couldn't hold back. The image of our juniors proudly defending Monty's 'cadet status' was too much, and the entire room burst into laughter. 'Push-ups *bhi karta hai!*' someone mocked, still laughing.

Monty's legacy didn't end there, though. If you left your almirah open, Monty would likely inspect it for you. It became second nature for us to keep our doors, windows, and almirahs firmly shut. But every once in a while, Monty would surprise someone.

But no matter how much trouble he caused, Monty was ours. He wasn't just a mouse—he was an AFPI legend. Outsiders could laugh, but no one could understand the bond we had with that giant, push-up-performing *chuha*. Monty wasn't just a mouse; Monty was an AFPI spirit in furry form.

◆◆◆

It was a quiet night, just past fall-in at 10 p.m. The mess had served its usual hearty meal, simple yet fulfilling, but some nights demand more than just satisfaction—they demand indulgence. That night, our hearts craved pizza, the cheesy, heavenly delight we could only dream about while enduring the Academy's disciplined routine. It wasn't just hunger; it was a calling.

The squad was assembled: me, DST, and Singla. The plan? A daring mission to smuggle pizzas from The Seventh Heaven, the new 24/7, the telephone room since the room reshuffling, near the tuck shop. The challenge? Guards on high alert after Lahsun and Mau's infamous night out escapades. But we were determined.

'Are you sure about this?' I asked, scanning the perimeter.

DST grinned. 'Sure? This is destiny.'

Singla, always the strategist, added, 'If we're going to do this, we have to be sharp. This isn't just a craving—it's an operation.'

The first obstacle was the Alpha Block guard. Singla, with his ever-reliable charm, approached him. With him was DST.

'Sir, I need to make an urgent call home,' Singla said, his voice low and respectful. 'It's really important.'

The guard narrowed his eyes. 'What's so urgent after fall-in? You cadets always have some excuse.'

'Sir, it's about some family matters. I wouldn't disturb you unless it was important,' Singla pleaded with such sincerity that even I almost believed him standing near the water cooler.

After a long pause, the guard relented. 'One minute. No more. And don't try anything funny.'

'Thank you, sir,' Singla said, almost bowing in gratitude.

He slipped into the Seventh Heaven, where he was supposed to 'call home'. Instead, he dialled me. Meanwhile, DST, like a ninja, sneaked out of the window and headed towards the wall. From my position on the first floor of the Alpha Block, I answered the call.

'Reporting in,' Singla whispered dramatically. 'DST is moving towards the wall. The guard is stationed near the basketball court. I repeat, the guard is stationary. Over.'

I chuckled. 'Got it. Is the delivery boy there?'

'Negative. But DST is crouching like some kind of action hero. He's near the wall now.'

Meanwhile, DST was moving like he was in a spy movie, darting from shadow to shadow. The delivery boy arrived just as DST reached the wall. The pizzas were exchanged swiftly, and DST sprinted back towards the Seventh Heaven.

'Package secured,' Singla reported as he 'monitored' from the 24/7 corner. 'DST is returning to base.'

From my position, I dropped our makeshift belt rope with my bag hanging on it. DST stuffed the pizzas into the bag, and I hauled it up like a fisherman reeling in his catch while Singla and DST returned to their rooms unsuspected by the guard.

We stashed the pizzas in Lahsun's room—our trusty hideout. Lahsun himself was on yet another night out with his eternal partner-in-crime, Mau and Moan, so we had the room to ourselves. We laid out our feast like kings, laughing and munching away.

Just as we were halfway through, DST muttered, 'You know, if we get caught, this is going to cost us at least 20 ETs each.'

Singla waved him off. 'Relax. If we get caught, it'll probably get Lahsun some company. That guy practically lives in ET mode.'

The best part? We weren't caught. Not a single guard suspected a thing. Lahsun returned the next morning, grinning ear to ear from his own adventures. He didn't even flinch when we told him we had turned his room into Pizza HQ.

'Good job,' he said, nodding approvingly. 'But next time, call me. I'm the expert.'

True to his reputation, Lahsun didn't learn from his past mistakes. A week later, he was back at it again with Mau and Moan, scaling walls and sneaking out like it was a sport.

◆◆◆

Room No. 12 was where legends were born and rules were tested. With most windows sealed to curb night-outs, Mau's bathroom window—unsealed during his holiday—became the secret gateway to freedom. It wasn't just a bathroom window anymore; it was our lifeline for covert missions, and tonight, it was the stage for another Operation Pizza Craving.

It was past fall-in, and the Academy was silent. But our cravings were loud. I, Madhira, Mau, and 'Aqua Man' (he hailed from Haryana, giving him the name for the sheer lack of water) knew that the mess food wasn't the issue—it was the desire for something cheesy and greasy.

'Mau,' I whispered, 'your bathroom window is back in action tonight. We're ordering pizzas.'

Mau raised an eyebrow. 'Do I look like a delivery agent to you?'

'No,' Aqua cut in, smirking, 'you look like someone who can still fit through that window.'

With a dramatic sigh, Mau gave in. 'Fine. But this better be worth it.'

The plan was simple: Mau and Aqua would go to the wall to receive the pizzas, while Madhira and I, our 'mission control', would stay back, coordinating via boots. Aqua, ever the optimist, declared, 'This is going to be smoother than butter.'

With practised efficiency, Mau and Aqua squeezed through the bathroom window, one after the other. Mau, however, didn't make a graceful landing. There was a loud thud, followed by his muffled groan.

'What now?' I hissed through the phone.

'Mau got ambushed!' Aqua whispered, barely holding in laughter.

'Ambushed?!'

'Yes, by a football stand!' Aqua explained. 'It just… attacked him!'

'Mau,' I snapped, 'how can a stationary object attack you?'

'It was hiding in the dark!' Mau groaned dramatically.

Madhira, listening in, burst into laughter. 'Tell him to stop whining and start walking. This is a mission, not a field trip!'

Despite his 'injury', Mau trudged on, Aqua supporting him. When they reached the wall, I directed them via phone.

'Delivery ETA (Estimated Time of Arrival) two minutes,' I said. 'Stay low. No sudden movements.'

As the delivery guy approached, Aqua whispered, 'He's here. Let's grab the pizzas and head back.'

Everything seemed fine—until it wasn't.

From the phone, I heard the delivery guy shout, 'What's going on?! Who are you people?!'

'What's happening?' I demanded.

'The guy panicked!' Aqua whispered furiously. 'He's backing away! He thinks we're after him!'

Before I could respond, the delivery guy bolted, pizzas in hand, yelling, 'I'm not delivering here again!'

Back in the room, Madhira and I stared at each other in stunned silence. 'What now?' he asked.

'We order again,' I said firmly. 'No mission fails on my watch.'

The second attempt was smoother. The pizzas were smuggled through the same bathroom window, and the operation concluded with a feast in Mau's room. Mau, of course, grumbled about the mess we made.

'This better not become a habit,' he muttered, biting into his slice.

'Oh, it will,' Aqua quipped. 'You've got the best escape route in the block!'

The best part? We never got caught, at least not for this mission. Mau, undeterred by the night's chaos, soon found himself planning more escapades, often with his infamous partner-in-crime, Moan. And as for the delivery guy? Well, he probably still tells stories about the two shadowy figures who 'ambushed' him that night.

◆◆◆

A few days after the incident, an officer from the Pioneer course visited us. As he stood before us, his presence demanded attention. Without wasting time, he began sharing his journey, taking us back to when AFPI was far more challenging than we could imagine. 'There was no tuck shop like today,' he said. 'We made do with room No. 1 for snacks and room No. 2 for laundry. It wasn't easy, but we endured. And yet, despite all that, I failed to make it to the NDA—not because of my ability, but because of my own mistakes.'

His words hit hard, but his next statement cut deeper. 'I don't want you to carry the burden I do,' he said, his voice firm. 'You're like my younger brothers, so I'll be honest with you. If you think you'll get recommended without giving it your absolute best, you're wrong. And if you think you can afford even one reckless decision, let me tell you—regret doesn't forgive.'

He paused, letting the silence drive his point home. 'If you step outside these walls for a night out, thinking it's just once, you're playing with fire. It won't stop at once. And if, God forbid, you fail, knowing it was because of that one mistake, that regret will live with you forever. It will crush you.'

His eyes scanned the room, every word deliberate. 'These walls are not restrictions; they are here to protect you. Within them, you can fall, learn, and grow. Outside, the world won't give you that chance. Choose wisely because the decisions you make here will define the rest of your life.'

That day, he didn't just speak; he made us feel the weight of our choices. Every word stayed with us—a reminder that discipline isn't a rule; it's a responsibility.

Then, with a slight smile, he added, 'When I was out there preparing for the CDS, I learned something invaluable. Even if some of us don't enter the Armed Forces, the character development we experience at AFPI moulds us into gentlemen of society. People look up to us and say, "You've been prepared amazingly," for we carry with us the values of discipline, integrity, and leadership that AFPI instils in each of its cadets. These qualities will remain with us, regardless of the paths we take in life.'

Dreams Gateway

Surya ast, Bahuguna mast!
—*CO Bahuguna Sahab, Impact*

Ultimately, the day of the written examination arrived—the day we had all been waiting for after months of relentless training. The air was thick with anticipation, yet it carried a sense of pride. I can still picture those days vividly—borrowing Sariya's ultimate GK book, only to find him doing front rolls in the squadron line, paying the price for stealing a nap, or watching Boobik, half-hanging off the bed and half on a chair, burning the midnight oil.

Then, there was Doda, my next-room partner, who had his own unique way of coping with exhaustion. Every night, around 2:00 or 3:00 a.m., he would shuffle into my room, half-asleep, and say, 'Shivam, I'm sleeping on your bed for 15 minutes. Wake me up after that.' It became a routine—15 minutes of stolen rest amidst hours of gruelling preparation. These were just a few of the many stories of perseverance in our squadron, each cadet pushing themselves harder than they ever thought possible, united by a shared goal—to make it.

'Alright, gentlemen,' I recalled Bahuguna Sir's statement, 'Now it's time to celebrate... or cry, depending on your results of written.'

A board was set up just outside the MVH, where juniors left their heartfelt messages for us. The messages were moving enough to run another layer of determination through the Titans, building the confidence we all needed just before D-Day.

◆◆◆

The morning of the exam was electric. Everyone was up at 5:00 a.m. sharp, dressed in our crisp Muftis, and ready to face the challenge ahead. But what truly made that day unforgettable was the gesture from the Tigers. Like family, they went room to room, carrying home-baked cakes and chocolates, wishing us luck with genuine warmth. At that moment, it didn't feel like we were in an Academy—it felt like home. Their words of encouragement weren't just wishes; they were reminders of the legacy we were expected to carry forward, a legacy rooted in pride, determination, and brotherhood.

Before heading out, we gathered in the fall-in area for a small prayer to Waheguru. There was silence as we bowed our heads, asking for strength, clarity, and the courage to do our best. It wasn't just about the exam—it was about proving to ourselves that we were ready to take one step closer to our dreams.

With smiles on our faces and a tinge of nervousness in our hearts, we boarded the bus to the examination centre. The atmosphere was charged with josh, and as the bus pulled away, we shouted in unison, '*Nishchay Kar Apni Jeet Karoon!*' It wasn't just a slogan; it was a promise to ourselves and to each other that we wouldn't back down.

That day, we weren't just cadets sitting for an exam—we were warriors marching towards our dreams.

Singla, Rishi, Gaint, and I were assigned to the same examination centre, while Sariya's was a bit further away. The day began with a sense of unity as we all set out together. After being dropped at a common location, we made sure to accompany Sariya to his centre, navigating through unfamiliar streets to find his centre. Once he was settled, we returned to our own centre, ready to face the challenge ahead.

The first paper was Mathematics. The hall was silent, yet the pressure was deafening. Every cadet was lost in their own battle with the questions in front of them. As I handed in my paper, a wave of doubt crept over me—my performance wasn't up to the mark, and I knew it. The unease followed me out of the hall, lingering as we gathered for lunch.

Sensing my silence, Gaint stepped forward. Acting like the true leader he was, he placed a reassuring hand on my shoulder. 'Shivam,' he said firmly, 'I know this isn't what you expected, and maybe it didn't go as well as you wanted. But now, focus. What's done is done. GAT (General Aptitude Test) is still ahead, and that's your chance. If you even manage to scrape through Maths, GAT will pull you up in merit. Don't let one exam dictate your entire performance. Pick yourself up—this is your time.'

His words hit me like a bolt of energy. He wasn't just consoling me; he was reminding me of my strength, urging me to keep fighting. It was leadership at its finest—lifting someone when they felt defeated, not letting them give in to self-doubt.

Motivated and refocused, I walked into the GAT exam with a new mindset. This was my shot, and I wasn't going to let it slip away. The hours flew by, and when I finally handed in my paper, there was a sense of redemption.

By 5:30 p.m., we were back at the Academy, a mix of relief and optimism in the air. While the Maths paper had been a hurdle for some, the GAT gave everyone a renewed sense of hope.

At 6:00 p.m., cadets began heading home. For many, this was the first time in months they'd see their families—parents they hadn't hugged in over half a year.

The joy of going home was unmatched, but as I watched the juniors standing tall, ready to take on their roles in our absence, a bittersweet pride filled me. It was their time to step into the spotlight and carry the weight of the Academy's expectations.

◆◆◆

After a week of warmth, homemade meals, and cherished family time, we returned to the Academy with renewed energy. The gates welcomed us back to the grind. PT in the morning under the ever-watchful eyes of Rajinder Sahab, school, lunch, and then 'games'—although the word didn't do justice to the gruelling sessions disguised as sports. Rajinder Sahab's obsession with PT ensured that games felt more like just another PT session. But amidst all the routine, something had changed.

There was a sudden surge in enthusiasm to hit the gym. Each of us wanted to carve out the best versions of ourselves, to transform into the charming men we dreamed of being. After all, we'd be back at school soon, and the teenage energy within us demanded we stand out, becoming the stars for every girl's attention. The mirrors of the Academy gym had never reflected so much determination, though, deep down, we all knew that somewhere, it was just a distraction from what was coming—the NDA written result.

The days dragged on as we waited. Every trip to the MVH was filled with anticipation, only to return with frustration when there was no news. The wait gnawed at our patience. Each joke about the result being out felt crueller than the last. The pranks kept growing, with people racing to the MVH to check the UPSC (Union Public Service Commission) site until the fateful evening of 26 September 2023, the day that would etch itself in my memory forever.

That evening, the Academy was buzzing with the final basketball match between Bravo and Charlie. Cheers filled the air as the Cheetahs claimed victory, but amidst the celebrations, someone shouted, 'Result *aa gya!*' The court fell silent for a moment, then erupted in chaos. We all rushed to MVH. My heart raced as I entered the room and requested someone to check my roll number.

The verdict hit me like a hammer: I hadn't made it.

I stood there, the world around me growing distant. The cheers of those who had cleared echoed in the background, but for me, time froze. My understudy, someone I hadn't interacted much with until now, came running, joy dancing on his face. 'Sir, *aapka ho gaya na?*' he asked, his eyes shining with hope.

With all the strength I could muster, I forced a smile and replied, 'I'm sorry, bro… I couldn't.' His face fell, and for a moment, I saw my own reflection in his disappointment—the same heartbreak I had felt when my OD couldn't make it.

In that silence, my understudy—Param—spoke up, though I could sense that his words were laced with the care and respect due to a senior. 'Sir, there will be moments when you might falter and when you feel like everything's falling apart. But remember this: When an AFPIan falls, he still falls into place. Every failure, every setback, is part of the larger plan to make you stronger. Never let these moments define you. Rise again, fight harder, and prove your mettle.'

His words, although a tad too empathetic for my taste, carried a sincerity that I couldn't help but appreciate. They were like a gentle push, not overbearing, yet filled with enough care to remind me of the resilience that lies within.

Back in my room, the walls seemed to close in. That's when Atma Sir walked in. He didn't say much; he didn't need to. With his calm demeanour, he simply asked, 'You okay?' I nodded, though my throat tightened, and my heart felt like it was sinking. He gave me a reassuring pat on the back and left.

The moment he stepped out, 'Lul' entered, followed by Thakur. Lul didn't say a word; he just wrapped me in a hug. It was the kind of hug that speaks louder than words, one that says, 'I'm here, and it's okay to let it out.' I couldn't hold back anymore—the tears flowed. 'It's just five marks in Maths, ten in total,' I mumbled through sobs, 'but even one mark counts, doesn't it?'

Lul tightened his grip. 'Bro, it's not the end. You're a Titan, and after all, you're an AFPIan, and AFPIans don't fall forever. We stumble, we learn, and we rise again. This isn't your last fight.'

Thakur chimed in, his voice steady but with a hint of shared pain, 'We've all seen how hard you worked, Shivam. Maybe this wasn't your time, but your time will come. Mark my words.' He paused for a moment, then added with a faint smile, 'I didn't make it either, bro. But that doesn't mean we stop here. This is just a step back to leap forward. The world doesn't end here—it begins. Let's push harder together. We owe it to ourselves to show everyone, and most importantly to ourselves, what we're truly capable of.'

His words, laced with both empathy and determination, lifted a heavy weight off my chest. It was at that moment that I realised—this journey wasn't just mine. It was ours, and we would rise again together.

As the night wore on, my Titans rallied around me, not letting me sink into despair. Each of them, whether they had cleared or not, showed unwavering camaraderie.

Yes, the pain of not making it stung deeply, but it was a lesson in resilience. I knew my hard work had fallen short this time, but I also knew that this wasn't the end of my story. It was just the beginning of a new chapter—a chapter where I would rise stronger, work harder, and prove that a Titan never gives up and I AM AN AFPIan.

I had been shutting everyone out, ignoring everyone at school, consumed by my own thoughts. But then, Ms Birinder approached me. With her gentle but firm voice, she called me aside and said, 'Failures are not the end, Shivam. They are lessons. You now know where you fell short, and you know how to bridge that gap. This experience will make you stronger. Trust the process.'

As I stood there, her words lingered, not offering immediate relief but a sense of calm in the midst of my confusion.

◆◆◆

Out of 46, 35 of The Titans had made it through—a historic achievement for AFPI, a record-breaking number that would forever be etched in its legacy. I was genuinely happy for my brothers, each one of them. Watching their names being celebrated, seeing their smiles and hearing their cheers brought a strange mix of emotions. They had earned it, and I felt proud to have been part of this remarkable batch. Yet, amidst the celebrations, I couldn't escape the pang of regret that clung to me, knowing I wasn't among them.

What moved me most was the quiet solidarity they showed. Despite their joy, there was no grand celebration, no loud cheers meant to overshadow those who didn't make it. Their triumph wasn't just for themselves; it was for all of us, a shared moment of pride.

The bond we shared as Titans was unshakable. That day, they taught me what brotherhood truly meant—not just in shared successes but in standing together, lifting those who stumbled, and reminding them that the journey was far from over. It wasn't just their victory; it was ours. And though I didn't make it this time, their strength and unity gave me hope that someday, I, too, would earn my place beside them.

As I lay in bed that night, staring at the ceiling, I repeated to myself the words our Director Sir always said: 'I want to see all 46 of you at NDA.' I might not be there yet, but I promised myself that maybe not today, not tomorrow, but one day, I would earn the stars on my shoulders—not just as a symbol of rank but as a testament to my unwavering dream. Because no star in the sky can shine brighter than the ones I'll proudly wear, etched with the sweat, sacrifice, and determination that will carry me there.

The Law of Unstable Equilibrium

I totally disagree with you!!!

Packed with energy and anticipation, the SSB classes began, transforming life into a whirlwind of discipline, humour, and utter chaos. The 35 moving from one class to another, grabbing onto computers to fill in their brain banks with as much information as possible. The rest of us? Some had gone home on mysterious 'urgent leaves', and others were hidden away in their cabins, either pretending to study or discussing how to convince the director to send us on leave. The ones in the cabins were the real intellectuals, though—deep in debates about 'whether shoes polished with toothpaste look shinier'.

And then, the word was introduced: 'gentleman'. The moment our instructor used it, it was like he had unleashed a nuclear idea. Suddenly, it became the most overused word in our dictionary. Every guy in the batch started inserting it into conversations unnecessarily.

'Gentleman, pass me the water.'

'Gentleman, your tie is crooked.'

'Gentleman, who took my snacks?!'

It got so bad that one guy stubbed his toe on a table and yelled, 'Gentleman, ouch!' You couldn't escape it. If someone sneezed, the entire group would collectively bless them with, 'Gentleman, bless you.' It was a pandemic.

One day, Bakra—the guy who always had something dramatic to say—walked into the mess, looked at his plate, and announced loudly, 'Gentleman, this *dal* has been crafted by the gods themselves!' Everyone burst out laughing, but not because of the comment—because even in humour, you never questioned the food in the Academy. The food was always the best.

The real comedy, though, was in the GTO (Group Testing Officer) classes. Our GTO Sir had his own theories about life, leadership, and winning group discussions. 'Never, ever say, "I totally disagree with you",' he warned, wagging his finger like a strict schoolmaster. 'Instead, say, "I partially agree with you." Gentleman, diplomacy is key!'

The GTO classes acted more like motivational sessions rather than GTO sessions. Our GTO Sir was always ready with a motivational video exclusively picked. From where? We don't know. The song *'O Sikandar'* boomed through the whole office area. The videos, along with his line 'Don't you all want to be coursemates at NDA too', renewed the energy.

He also loved metaphors. 'Be like a kingfisher,' he declared one day. 'Drop a point, observe, and then swoop back in with a stronger point, just like a kingfisher catching a fish.' The problem? The word 'kingfisher' had a very different connotation for most of us. Mau leaned over and whispered, 'Strong or Premium?' It took everything in us not to laugh out loud. The idea of discussing beer in a GTO class was hilarious, but we knew better than to say it out loud. One slip-up and sir would have turned us into actual kingfishers, diving into mud pits as punishment.

However, the most interesting part of the GTO was the individual obstacles, something that everyone just pretended to take very seriously. Even the guys who didn't clear the written exams would dive in as if their futures depended on walking across a plank or climbing a rope. But one day, things went from hilarious to horrifying in no time.

One of the obstacles among the tasks was the balance beam, basically three thin wooden logs that a person needed to walk on without holding onto anything and maintaining his balance.

On this day, Gulati was practising the balance beam, looking all determined like he was about to conquer the world. But destiny had other plans. Just as he stepped onto the beam, his balance decided to call in sick, and he slipped. What happened next was a masterpiece of tragic comedy: he fell with his legs spread wider than a compass, slamming his crown jewels straight onto the beam.

For a second, there was silence, the kind of silence where you could hear everyone's souls leave their bodies. Some guys bit their lips to stop laughing; others covered their mouths like they were at a funeral. But trust me, no one doubted the seriousness of the situation. His face contorted in pain, and we could almost hear his ancestors wailing in unison, mourning for the future generations that were now in serious jeopardy.

He was sent home for a few days to recover, but thankfully, nothing permanent happened. We still joked that if he had to write his SSB medical report, it would just say: 'Fought bravely but couldn't protect the family legacy.'

The interviewing officer was the silent one. What went inside his cabin? Only he and the cadet knew. But most of them would come out shaken about their lack of preparation and would be seen running to the MVH to google the questions. The psych was a visibly exhaustive task. I would look at them massaging their hands after the test, discussing the pictures and the words.

English-speaking classes were another goldmine of comedy. Twice a week, we were made to participate in activities that were supposed to improve our language skills. Most of the time, we ended up improving our ability to control laughter.

The highlight was the day Pomeranian was given the role of a girl in a role-play activity. To really sell the part, he folded his T-shirt collar inward to make it look like a deep-neck top and flipped his imaginary hair. Then, in the most exaggerated South Delhi accent, he began: 'Oh my God, Gentleman, like seriously? This tea tastes so… basic. I wanted Starbucks! Is this how you treat a lady?!'

The entire class erupted. Even our teacher had to turn around to hide her smile. Someone shouted, 'Gentleman, should we get him some earrings?'

◆◆◆

Ah, Sundays in the winters—the rare moments we cadets felt like kings. Sunshine was our saviour, and we'd lay our bedsheets near the obstacle course, soaking in the warmth like lizards basking in glory. It was pure bliss.

On one such Sunday, Moan and I were lounging in our sunny retreat when something extraordinary caught our eyes. Walking across the ground, bathed in golden sunlight, was someone in an Academy tracksuit—long, flowing hair, fair skin, and an elegance that made us both sit up straight.

'Bro,' I whispered to Moan, 'Is that... a girl?'

Moan squinted, frozen in shock. 'A girl? Here? In our Academy? What kind of miracle is this?'

Desperate for answers, I flagged down a junior, Nirbhik, who was passing by. 'Nirbhik!' I called, trying to sound casual but failing miserably. 'Who's that?' I gestured subtly toward the figure gliding across the ground like a shampoo commercial come to life.

Nirbhik took one look and started laughing—full-on, breathless laughter.

'That, sir,' he said between gasps, 'is Russian!'

'Russian?' I blinked, confused. 'What do you mean, Russian? What's a Russian doing here?'

He tried to catch his breath but couldn't stop grinning. 'No, sir, not a Russian. That's our Russian.'

Now, I was completely lost. 'What do you mean "our Russian"? Are you telling me we have a foreign exchange program no one told me about?'

Moan, who had been silently observing, suddenly burst into laughter, slapping his thigh. 'Man, you idiot! That's no Russian girl! That's one of the juniors. He has just opened his *jooda* to dry his hair!'

I froze, staring at the so-called 'Russian'. The realisation hit me like a sack of bricks. It wasn't some ethereal girl. It was a cadet casually drying his hair in the sun.

Moan, still laughing, clapped me on the back. 'You were ready to ask for her—oh, sorry, his—Instagram handle, weren't you?'

From that day on, the nickname 'Russian' stuck, and I learnt a very important lesson that appearances under the winter sun can be dangerously deceptive.

◆◆◆

Amidst all this chaos, birthdays never stopped. They just became wilder. It was Kirmada's birthday, and the man had finally turned 18. Kirmada's birthday somehow always meant doom, and so did this time too. This was no ordinary night—half the block was out celebrating while the other half pretended to be too sleepy to join the chaos. As soon as the clock struck 12:00 a.m., the block erupted with music, thanks to Gyani, who had proudly bought a *baaja* during Liberty. The sound was so loud it felt like the block had been converted into a *shaadi ka pandal.* Guys were dancing like there was no tomorrow—some were pulling off Govinda moves, and others were trying to look like Tiger Shroff but failing miserably.

Meanwhile, I was fast asleep, oblivious to the chaos, but my ever-so-chatty squadron mate, Lahsun, was still awake, shouting outside my door, 'Shivam *bhai ke aage koi bol sakta hai kya? Ayeee* Shivam *bhaiii!*' I could hear him laughing softly, clearly inspired by the latest Instagram trend, while I buried my head under the pillow, hoping for some peace.

Suddenly, the guards decided they'd had enough of this wedding-turned-block-party and called in the big boss—the warden. Normally, in situations like these, a fall-in would be declared, and the entire course would be punished. But this time, the warden decided to take a direct approach. The block fell silent as soon as his footsteps echoed through the corridors. He knocked on the first door, and poor Tatyaal was the unlucky one.

Tatyaal, the real hero of the night, put on an Oscar-worthy performance. With a perfect expression of sleep, he greeted the warden like he'd just woken up from a deep, peaceful slumber. The warden entered the room, suspicious, and started checking every corner—under the bed, inside the bathroom, behind the cupboard. Finding nothing, he began to leave, and Tatyaal, ever the smooth operator, started closing the door behind him.

But alas! No one knows what suddenly struck the warden that day. He suddenly turned back and yanked the curtains aside—and there they were. Gandhiji's three monkeys—Sooden, Joban, and Dada—huddled together outside the window, trying their best to become invisible. The warden's face was priceless as he wrote down their names in his little book and marched off without a word. The block felt like it had been spared… for now.

Morning PT, however, was a different story altogether. After the usual 5 km run, the PTI had a special surprise for us: a full-track front roll drill. As we rolled and tumbled across the ground like sacks of potatoes, the juniors were busy with their own drills. The PTI was in full form, and to Mau, he yelled, 'Which finger were you showing in the camera while dancing last night, huh?' Mau, trying to play innocent, stayed quiet, but the senior PTI wasn't having it. 'Don't worry! Today in the games period, I'll show you what that middle finger actually means!' Mau's face was a mix of regret and terror as the rest of us tried to stifle our laughter mid-front-roll.

By the time classes started, nobody could focus. The fear of what awaited us after school loomed large. And when we returned to the Academy, the real storm hit. A fall-in was called immediately, and we were asked to put our bags down. Then began an hour or more long session of rolling, running, and every other imaginable position. It was chaos, but the worst was yet to strike. When we returned back to the bags, we saw phones laid ahead of us like a second-hand mobile shop. Teji Sir, the driver, even found a suspicious book in a bag, opening which, he discovered a phone neatly hidden inside with cutouts made for it. The look on his face was like he had just uncovered a national treasure.

This ordeal led to a jackpot for the drill instructor—ten phones were found in total. Thirty cadets were put on ETs after the analysing of the camera recordings for at least fourteen days each, and seven of the major appointments were de-tabbed, including the BCC, SCC Charlie, CSMs of all squadrons and CQMs of both Alpha and Charlie. Yes, that's right, it was time for the appointment reshuffling of the Titans; sounds like a legacy, indeed.

I was lucky enough. My *boot* was hidden in a leather file that the PTI mistook for some harmless document file. My heart was pounding so hard it felt like it could power the entire Academy. But as soon as I was cleared, I made a mental note to find a safer hiding spot next time.

But then... came Sant, the legend and the subject of all mischiefs.

With a completely straight face, the instructor reached into his bag and pulled out—wait for it—a hammer. Yes, a hammer. Now, Sant, looking just as shocked as the rest of us, froze for a moment. His eyes widened, and it was clear that he was about to get a whole lot of questions. How the heck did a hammer end up in his bag?

He stammered, 'Sir, I... I don't know how it got in there.' He was genuinely terrified, thinking he was about to be accused of hiding something way more sinister than a simple tool. I mean, who even carries a hammer in their bag? But as the staff stood there, scratching their heads, the whole room was tense—until the truth came out.

It turned out that Madhira, the resident prankster and class troublemaker, had discovered the hammer earlier that day. It had been left behind by a worker, and instead of doing the sensible thing (like returning it), Madhira did what only he would: he slipped it into Sant's bag. He forgot about it completely, of course, because why would anyone notice a hammer in a bag until it's pulled out during a staff bag check?

So, when the PTI pulled that hammer out, it was like a scene from a slapstick comedy. The staff were staring, Sant was sweating bullets, and the rest of us were trying to hold back our laughter. But then, the real kicker: Sant, completely unaware of the prank, was officially dubbed 'Thor'. The hammer was his new weapon, and it stuck, getting him a week's suspension and twenty ETs.

Madhira, of course, was grinning from ear to ear in the background, having pulled off the perfect prank. Sant was now the proud, albeit confused, owner of the hammer and the title 'Thor'. Talk about an unexpected rise to power!

When we finally dragged ourselves back to the cabins, heated discussions broke out all around us. Some were blaming each other; others were just trying to figure out who snitched. Within an hour, a notice went up: five suspensions, 30 ETs, and almost every senior appointment gone.

As I lay in bed that night, completely drained, Lahsun piped up again outside my door, 'Shivam *bhai ke aage toh sab* fail *hai, waise kal ka* PT special *hoga, dekh lena!*' I couldn't help but laugh despite everything. Life in the Academy was brutal, but man, it was never boring.

◆◆◆

3 December, a night before the annual Military Literature Festival (MLF), was just another cold night at MVH when Moan, with his infamous knack for chaos, barged into the room with his 'masterplan' for a night out. '*Bhai,* tonight is the night. We'll go out and have the time of our lives,' he said, already brimming with confidence. Mau joined him almost immediately because, well, Mau had a knack for turning bad ideas into catastrophic adventures.

At first, no one else was interested. A night out? Boring. But when someone mentioned that the seniors from Double First were joining in (a night in and night out simultaneously!), the dynamic changed. A night in by itself is rare, but a night in and a night out together? It's like spotting two leg pieces while eating biryani in the mess. Today, of all days, the guard on duty was the terrifying Amali—the warden's right hand on legs.

After an hour of plotting and pep talks, even Aqua, the otherwise sensible one, joined the gang. Let me just say that this decision was either the biggest mistake of his life—or the beginning of the greatest story he'd ever tell in his whole life.

By 10 p.m., the seniors had snuck into the Academy for their night in. By 11:30 p.m., Moan and his gang, with the seniors, were already trying to figure out how to leave because, surprise, the guard was parked right next to the anteroom. The same door they had slithered in through was no longer an option. That's when they decided to explore the first floor, looking for new 'creative exits'.

And then it happened.

They knocked on my door—Room 32. Half-asleep, I grumbled my way to the door, thinking it was some junior wanting notes or a charger. But when I opened it, my jaw dropped. Standing there, in a perfect formation, were ten seniors—enough to trigger my muscle memory into standing at attention and blurting out, 'Good evening, sir!' For a split second, it felt like I was back in my junior term, mentally going through my 'best excuses for punishment' list.

But the seniors were casual. '*Arre* Shivam, *kaisa hai*?' one asked as if this were a routine room visit. I stammered, 'Great, sir… uh, how about you?'

They ignored my awkwardness, marched to the windows, and flung them open. The cold winter air blasted into the room, and my poor mate, Pomeranian, for his love of warmth, immediately curled into my blanket like a burrito. After what felt like an eternity of arguing and brainstorming, the seniors decided that my room wasn't ideal for their escape and moved to Room 17. From there, they executed 'Operation Rooftop', sneaking out onto the mess roof like it was Mission Impossible.

I tried going back to sleep, but the warmth of my bed was gone—both literally and metaphorically. I muttered under my breath, 'Why me, guys? Why?'

But the real chaos started at midnight.

The hooter went off. That dreaded hooter, which had the uncanny ability to wake even the heaviest of sleepers. My first thought was, 'Seniors have been caught. Game over.' But when I reached the fall-in area, I saw Aqua standing alone, wearing his most miserable 'I messed up' face, surrounded by the entire course and juniors who had gathered to witness the spectacle.

The situation was grim. The warden had caught Aqua, and what followed was what we can only call a public slaughter. But our course wasn't having it. In a display of unity, we all refused to leave Aqua alone and staged a mini-strike. That's when the warden cracked and called in the big gun. The director.

Five minutes later, the director arrived in full force. And within minutes, he proved why he was a damn major general. He didn't yell. He didn't scream. He just took us aside to the tuck shop area, far from the juniors, and spoke calmly yet firmly. 'Guys,' he started, 'I know he made a mistake. I get it. But this behaviour… this isn't how things work.'

Now, here's where it got tricky. The director started asking questions about the plan. 'Where were you going? Who was involved? What was the budget? And why in God's name were you going to watch Sam Bahadur of all things?!'

To everyone's surprise, the director chuckled. 'You planned an entire operation for a military movie?' he said. 'I hope your future operations in the Armed Forces are just as… detailed.'

As a parting gift, he reinstated the MLF trip, which had been previously cancelled due to 'these behavioural issues'. This gesture made everyone cheer—for about 30 seconds—before the cursing of Moan and Mau resumed.

As for the seniors? They successfully snuck out of the Academy. The guards were too busy with the fall-in area to notice them sneaking out through the office wing. But by morning, the camera footage revealed everything. Because, as I've learned, you never, ever doubt the AFPI surveillance system.

As I was climbing the stairs back to my room, utterly drained from the whole ordeal, my buddy walked alongside me, smirking as if he'd just watched the best comedy of his life. With a sly grin, he said, 'Buddy *yaar,* seniors *ke* plans *ke chakkar mein tera* room *toh* crime scene *ban gaya hai. Dekh lena, kal tak tere* room *ke* windows *bhi* seal *kar denge, aur bahar* "Most Wanted" *ka* poster *chipka denge!*'

I couldn't help but laugh at the absurdity of it all, even though I was completely exhausted. It was the perfect end to the craziest night—a disaster for sure, but one hell of a story to tell.

Tech Hack

Kis kis ke paas phone hai? Khud hi btado!
—Warden Sahab

Everything seemed perfectly calm in the chilly winter air at the Academy, whispers barely audible—until we were handed our mobile phones. They were supposedly for 'studying'. Yeah, right. The juniors got their phones, too, but the irony? It was hard to ignore. These phones were supposed to be tools for academic excellence, but what we actually used them for was anything but studying. While we were supposed to be sharpening our minds, most of us found a much more exhilarating way to 'study'—mobile gaming. But here's the kicker—none of the seniors were ever caught. Why? Because we had perfected the art of sitting in our cabins, 'boots' firmly on, pretending to study while secretly hiding behind our screens, making every possible mistake in the book but doing it quietly.

It was an unspoken rule—don't get caught. And trust me, none of us did.

The comedy of it all was magnified by Singla and Guruji, the perfect buddy pair. These two were the supposed 'gods' of mobile phone management. Their sacred duty was to collect and distribute phones. The irony? Among the phones caught after Kirmada's birthday was Singla's own phone, with the warden taunting him with the now iconic line, '*Bharosa tod dia mera*'. The most absurd part? Most of us had a 'boot' secretly stashed in our rooms. The only exception to it may be was Rishi, who was as pure as his name. Whereas Sant, let's just not talk about him. And then there was Sal, Sal Sharma. This guy looked like the most innocent person you could imagine who could do nothing wrong. Yet, he was among those whose phones were caught, and since then, the warden couldn't stop taunting him.

Now, weeks after the mass course detabbing, the names of the new appointments popped up on the notice board, with the highlights being unexpected names like the new Alpha CSM Singla and BCA Guruji, the iconic buddy pair. For Guruji, it was the most expected thing, as the only reason he had not become the BCA last time was due to his swimming, which he had improved a thousand-fold by now, whereas Singla? This guy was on ETs among the mass detabbing, yet his name landed on the appointments notice. Why? Only the director knows.

But let's focus on the juniors for a minute. The moment they got their phones, it was like a modelling agency had opened up on the rooftop of the mess. They started clicking photos left and right as if the world had just discovered their perfect selfies. And, oh, the quotes. Every photo came with some motivational line, like 'Be the reason someone smiles today'. We'd all gather around, snickering behind, because honestly, they should have checked their own faces first before posting such 'inspirational' content. But no, every photo was uploaded with the quote and made into an Instagram story. And the worst part? They thought it was aesthetic and classy.

Meanwhile, the seniors had their own little tech hacks going on. While the juniors were busy posing, we were making use of real technological opportunities. Some of us had laptops submitted to the Academy, so we had the perfect excuse to hang out in the lecture halls. Why? Because the Wi-Fi was top-notch, so why study when you could game? And let me tell you, the gaming sessions were legendary. Smashcarts, anyone? That game ruled our computer world. Each of us raced to grab hold of our laptops or the computers in the MVH as soon as fall-in ended to take part in them.

Now, let's talk about the PA committee. They were the ones who had the ultimate power when it came to tech stuff. Their main job was ensuring all the computers were working, setting up PVHs for lectures, and managing everything that involved tech. And here's the thing: Singla and Guruji were the committee members. These two had the passwords to every computer and Wi-Fi network. Need access to anything? They were the gods you prayed to. And when we needed to use a camera for some photos during interviews, guess who turned into the strictest gatekeepers? That's right—Singla and Guruji. They'd turn us down every time, saying, 'You'll break it, like you always do,' as if we were toddlers playing with their toys (but to be fair, the camera was worth a lakh, nothing to be toyed with). Meanwhile, Guruji couldn't even take a decent photo to save his life, but he was the one with the camera.

And let's not forget when Singla, Anda, NSG, and I were working on the next edition of the Academy's annual magazine, *Boots and Saddles*. We reserved a computer for our project, but guess what? Singla had a habit of 'misusing' his privileges. He'd look at the guy sitting at the computer and say, 'Man, stand up. I need to use the computer for the magazine,' and then he'd proceed to start a game. And what could others do? Nothing.

But the real kicker came when the director finally had enough. One day, he declared, 'That's it. No more mobile phones. You're all wasting time and not studying.' His reason? Apparently, Bahuguna Sir had informed him that we were using our phones for, well, other things—ahem, incognito sites. For a moment, we were stunned. Did he really just say that? But yes, the mobile phones were confiscated, and we were all left to face the consequences of our actions.

But you know what? The 'boots' were always there. Always. Even without our phones, the Academy somehow found a way to keep us busy—and we, in turn, found a way to keep our 'boots' stashed away, ready for the next round of 'studying'. It was a cycle, a dance of tech, discipline, and, let's be honest, a lot of hiding behind screens. The Academy never stood a chance against our tech hacks. And neither did we.

◆◆◆

So, here's the thing: we are living in the gym freak era now. And trust me, the gym isn't just about flexing muscles; it's about proving a point! After Rishi roasted me like I was a piece of chicken on the grill, I decided to step up my game. I mean, the dude didn't even stop to breathe as he went on about how my understudy was crushing it at the higher tests while I was just... existing. 'Bro, learn something from your understudy. He is doing better than you!' Ouch. It was like the guy poured hot sauce into a wound I didn't even know existed.

That moment lit a fire inside me, the kind you get when someone calls you out in front of the whole squad. So, I straight up hit the gym like I was on a mission from the gods. I spent two months grinding. Chin-ups? They were still like a bad relationship—no matter how hard I tried, they just rejected me. I would almost make it, and then bam! The test day came, and it was like, 'Sorry Shivam, we can't be seen together in public. We're just secret friends.' Bro, seriously? I put in the effort, the sweat, and the tears. And all I got was rejection, just like trying to slide into a girl's DMs (Direct Messages) and getting left on read.

But when it came to everything else, I was killing it! Toe touch? Nailed it. Rope climbing? Easy! But chin-ups? Oh no, they were my Kryptonite.

Then came the day of the new test: shuttle runs. The PTI told us to line up, and suddenly... chaos. The Alpha Squadron was all confused. Nobody knew who was doing what. Who's counting? Who's running? Everyone just stared at each other like, 'What do we do now?' The director, of course, was like 'boom'—angry mode activated. He immediately declared the entire Alpha Squad a failure! Just like that. Doomed. Meanwhile, every other squadron managed to get their act together, but Alpha? We were too busy figuring out who should be counting, who should be running, and who should be in charge of looking confused.

It was like planning a military operation where everyone wanted to be the General but no one wanted to follow orders. So, there we were: the Alpha Squadron, the champions of failure. Just another day in the life of a wannabe gym freak.

Bunks & Battles

Haan, mai Tango Squadron ka coach tha!
—Mister Manoj, Shemrock

Enthralled by the excitement, the annual Shemrock Sports Meet was no ordinary event. It was our mini-Olympics, a battlefield of talent, and, for some of us, a golden opportunity to wreak havoc. This year, the event was held at a sprawling ground far away from the prying eyes of the principal and teachers—bliss. But with great freedom comes even greater stupidity, and trust Mau and me to grab it by the horns.

It all started during the lunch break on practice day. The sun was scorching, the ground dusty, and our energy levels dangerously low. Mau and I sat under the shade of a tree with our small gang of juniors. The conversation, like always, spiralled into madness.

'Bro, I'm starving,' Mau groaned, clutching his stomach dramatically.

'Eat the samosas from the school canteen stall,' I suggested.

Mau shot me a look like I'd just insulted his ancestors. 'Those samosas taste like cardboard dipped in used oil.'

'That's because they are, sir,' a junior chimed in.

Mau perked up suddenly, eyes glinting with mischief. 'You know what we need? Pizza.'

'Pizza?' I asked, raising an eyebrow.

'Yes, sir! Imagine hot, cheesy pizza with that tangy oregano seasoning,' one of the juniors said, practically drooling.

Another junior gasped. 'Are you crazy, sir? If Seema Ma'am finds out, she'll roast us alive!'

'Relax,' Mau said, waving dismissively. 'We'll order it online and pick it up quietly. Shivam, you're in, right?'

Now, my brain screamed, 'No, Shivam! This is trouble! Abort mission!' But my stomach growled louder. 'Okay, fine. But if we get caught, only we two are taking the blame, not them.'

'Deal!' Mau said, grinning.

Then came the real deal: logistics.

Mau announced. 'The plan is on. We need to pool money. Everyone chip in!'

All of us silently stared at him—the response to his command.

That's when Mau chimed in with a mischievous grin, 'Alright, consider it a belated birthday party from my side—my birthday was just a few days ago, after all.'

The plan was flawless—on paper. Mau and I convinced Birinder Ma'am that we needed extra practice for hosting.

'Ma'am,' I said with my best innocent face, 'we just want to ensure everything is perfect for tomorrow. We'll only take a few juniors involved in escorting the guest.'

She sighed but agreed. 'Fine, Shivam. But don't make me regret this.'

We snuck out of the ground like spies in a low-budget thriller. Mau, clutching the pizza delivery bag, looked like a smuggler in training.

Now, like every other plan where Mau was involved, one of the teachers caught us red-handed. Mau panicked, shoving his phone and the order bag to my understudy.

We told Param, 'Just run! She's never seen us before; she won't recognise you.' But as soon as the teacher shouted 'Stop!' Param froze, and like clockwork, he obeyed—two steps in, and he just stopped, handing over the bag like a perfect soldier.

Mau, ever the genius, blurted out, 'Tiffin, ma'am. Homemade.'

'Homemade? It smells like Domino's!' she snapped, snatching the bag.

And just like that, the pizzas were confiscated. We trudged back to the ground, defeated.

Later, we trudged back to school, where Seema Ma'am was waiting. 'Shivam!' she thundered. 'I told you not to take Mau!'

'Mistake is 50-50, ma'am,' I tried to reason.

'It's more like 70-30,' she snapped.

'Okay, ma'am, 70 mine, 30 his,' I said with a sheepish grin. Mau laughed, but ma'am didn't find it funny.

Seema Ma'am shook her head. 'Shivam, you're like a magnet for chaos. Why do you always take the fall for everyone?'

'It's a habit, ma'am,' I said with a grin.

After profuse apologies, she finally decided to return Mau's phone to his parents but declared the confiscated pizzas. Birinder Ma'am, our English teacher, tried to save us and added, 'It's their first mistake, ma'am. Let it go.'

Seema Ma'am reluctantly relented. 'Fine, no action from the Academy. But Shivam, this is your last chance.' I gave her my best 'puppy eyes of gratitude' look, which probably saved us.

◆◆◆

As if the pizza fiasco wasn't enough, day 1 of the sports meet brought fresh trouble. The four juniors were sent to escort the chief guest but ended up in the wrong section of the ground. The chief guest had to find his own way to the stage.

A teacher approached me with a stern look, 'Shivam, where are your juniors? It was a mistake today, and I'll let it slide, but tomorrow—don't let this happen again.' For a moment, I stood there, nodding like a responsible senior, 'Okay, ma'am, it's my responsibility.' But just as I was about to take in the gravity of the situation, a pizza box appeared right in front of me. I froze. 'Ma'am, please don't put this on me. If anything goes wrong tomorrow, I swear I'm not taking the fall for this!' She burst out laughing, shook her head, and walked away, leaving me there, torn between guilt and sheer relief.

On day 2, the sports meet was wild. The director was the chief guest; everyone went full throttle in events and chaos was everywhere. But the real fun started when it was my turn to run the 800m. I was co-hosting with Mau, and just as I was about to leave the stage, Mau, all hyped up, shouted, 'Shivam Sharma, leaving the stage to run for his house!' I had no choice but to dash off, throwing on shorts and looking like a mess.

As I was preparing to leave, Mau was right there, giving me motivational pumps like, 'Go, Shivam! You got this!' But I knew deep down I was about to get wrecked. I ran like I was on fire but came in fifth—total disaster.

But here's the best part: as I crossed the finish line, I passed by the hosting area where the director was sitting.

He casually said, 'Shivam, you ran amazingly!' Mau, hearing that, went wild, shouting, 'Shivam was praised by the director!' and the whole Academy lost it. I wasn't the winner, but for a moment, I was the hero of the day!

◆◆◆

After the sports meet, an emotional wave hit us all. On usual days, we could never stand the way our PTI treated us—those gruelling punishments, the endless exercises, and the relentless drills. But today was different. It was the day of Rajinder Sahab's retirement. After serving at AFPI for eight glorious years, it was time for him to pass on the position. The morning PT was a symbolic one, with him joining us for the josh push-ups, which left us in awe about his fitness at this age. In the evening, we had a small party for him in the mess, and from the Twelfth course, we all chipped in to gift him a watch. Some of us recited poetry, and others mimicked his signature PTI style—every moment filled with joy, love, and respect.

The man who had been our toughest critic suddenly became the one we couldn't imagine our lives without. When we said, 'Sir, we will always miss the sound of your car in the morning,' everyone felt the weight of the words. That car, which we dreaded hearing because it meant PT, would no longer be a part of our mornings. The man had taught us so much more than just exercises; he had taught us discipline, respect, and the importance of pushing our limits.

A new PTI, Ramkishan Sir, came in to take his place, but for us Titans, no one could fill the shoes of Rajinder Sahab. The new PTI was great, no doubt, but the memories we had with the old one were irreplaceable. It felt like saying goodbye to a mentor, a guide, and a friend—someone who shaped us in ways we didn't fully realise until that moment.

◆◆◆

The new PTI was a character of his own—his style was unmatched. He wasn't just about drills; he'd go on about the history of PT—who invented it, when, why, and where; as if we were prepping for a history exam instead of breaking a sweat. But Rajinder Sahab was in a whole different league. He'd make you laugh even when you were gasping for air.

I remember one particular games period when I was running with my heavyweight friend Sachkirat. Now, overweight guys in PT rarely got to play. Their 'game' was endless running, sometimes with a five-kilo medicine ball for company. As we huffed and puffed our way around the track, the old PTI gave us his signature taunt: '*Jinko dekhne ke liye tum dhire daudte ho, woh bhi sochti hongi, kitne kamzor hain!*'

For a moment, I was utterly confused. '*Kaun dekhne ke liye*?' I thought. That's when Sachkirat, panting like a steam engine, turned to me and said, 'Bro, *woh* swimming *ke liye aayi hain... isi liye bol raha hai!*' I looked up, and there they were—the lady cadets from Mai Bhago Academy, here for their swimming lessons. It hit me like a truck. The old man wasn't just taunting us; he was roasting us alive. We shouted back, 'Sir, *hum waise wale ladke nahi hain!*' But we knew that the damage was done.

The new PTI, though, didn't deal in taunts. His focus was stunts. He'd do handstands, clap push-ups, and whatnot, all while barking commands. But when it came to running? That was still the sacred domain of Rajinder Sahab, the track king himself. No handstands could outrun that legend.

◆◆◆

It was our pre-board exams, and I was deep into my Physics paper when Neha Ma'am called me out. For a moment, my heart skipped a beat—was I caught cheating? But I wasn't even cheating! Nervously, I walked up to her, and instead of scolding me, she asked, 'Shivam, do you know how a search engine works on an iPhone?'

Before I could respond, Moan shouted from the back, 'Ma'am, it has Safari!' I quickly pointed at him and said, 'Ma'am, he's the rich man—you can ask him!'

Now, let me introduce you to Neha Ma'am—a teacher so involved in everything that sometimes you wonder if she has clones working in shifts. From conducting exams to catching students mid-mischief to setting the record straight on discipline, she's everywhere, all the time. Need someone to enforce the rules? Neha Ma'am. Need someone to enforce rules again because you broke them the first time? Still Neha Ma'am.

But she's not just the enforcer; she's also the saviour. Don't have your practical file on the last day of submission? Neha Ma'am to the rescue! She's the one who saved Dada when he lost his file on the very day of checking. In her signature style, she worked her magic, quickly arranging a file in front of the examiner while Dada stood there, sweating bullets.

Also, let me tell you, 'rich men' isn't just a phrase; it's practically a title of honour (out of sarcasm) bestowed by our beloved warden. Anytime someone flaunts their ultimate 'richness' or indulges in extraordinary expenses, the tag 'rich men' is thrown their way. Moan just happened to be the prime recipient that day, and honestly, I couldn't have been happier to deflect the spotlight onto him!

◆◆◆

After the pre-boards, everything felt different. Those who hadn't cleared the written exams were sent home, while the rest geared up for the final stretch of preparation for the SSB. The air was filled with a mix of anxiety and determination. But then, a mistake happened—a reckless one, not by us this time, but by our juniors. About ten of the tigers, driven by the madness of youth and the thrill of rebellion, decided to pull a night out. The staff, as expected, was kept in the dark. But, as fate would have it, they were caught. And the new PTI, true to his form, made sure they understood the gravity of their actions. The consequences were swift—their winter breaks were cancelled. The punishment, harsh and unforgiving, struck hard.

While we were back home for the holidays, it wasn't the usual excitement. The SSB candidates, now deep in their own journey, would call us daily. As we sat in the comfort of our homes, we heard stories from the Academy—stories of survival, of camaraderie. They told us how, at the end of days, they were watching movies on laptops, amazingly sneaked into the room, the last eight of them packed into a single room, mattresses thrown onto the floor to create a small, chaotic refuge. Meanwhile, our hearts ached with longing as we realised how much we missed the brothers—the family we had created there.

That month at home, though filled with love and warmth, felt incomplete. It was emotional in ways I can't describe. Every day felt like a countdown to a life we were soon going to leave behind. The thought of losing that sense of belonging, the laughter, the fights, the shared hardships, the inside jokes—everything that had become our home—was unbearable. We were growing up and moving on, but it didn't come without a heavy heart. The Fourteenth course was getting ready for their entrance exam, a reminder that change was inevitable, and soon, we would have to bid farewell to the place that had shaped us, to the brothers who had become a part of us.

It felt like we were on the verge of losing everything. But in the midst of that uncertainty, I understood something profoundly true: the Academy wasn't just a place. It was a home we had earned, a family we had built. And no matter where we went from there, those memories, those bonds, would never fade. They would always be a part of us, no matter how far apart we became.

◆◆◆

At this time now, the Academy was half empty. Some of the Titans had already returned home after their SSB, along with a few from us eleven, while others were still caught up in their own selection process. Every time we heard of a selection, it felt like a victory for us. When the first Titan, Sooden, was recommended, it filled us with the purest joy. It wasn't just his win—it felt like our win. But when we heard the news of not being selected, it felt like our own personal loss.

As the numbers dwindled, there were just a few left in the Academy. The atmosphere had changed. The once bustling halls were now quieter and emptier. Yet, in those smaller groups, a bond stronger than ever had formed. When everyone returned in January, with the final recommendation count of ten among the 35 that went for the SSBs, the Academy felt like home again despite its vastness. Rooms No. 17 and No. 32 became our sanctuary—eight of us packed together like one big family. No one wanted to sleep alone, not in a block where only a handful of us remained.

But despite being only eight, we had to go to school; no relief from there. But where there is misery, we AFPIans find a way to have fun.

That's when the ultimate plan hit us. Let's make another memory, Shemrock-style. And what could be more iconic than Spider-Man? Yes, the Spider-Man. Not the one slinging webs in New York but the Spider-Man statue perched on Shemrock School's rooftop—its very own unofficial mascot, watching over the campus like a silent guardian.

The plan was simple: climb to the roof, meet Spider-Man, and return. Kumbhkaran and I spearheaded the operation. Leaving the classroom with all the stealth of a Bollywood hero in a heist movie, we slipped past through a classroom door to the backyard like ninjas. Somewhere between the giggles and racing hearts, we found ourselves standing outside.

There it was—the staircase. It looked old and rusty, probably never meant for students, but to us, it screamed adventure. One by one, we climbed like warriors scaling a fortress, each step taking us closer to glory. And finally, there we were—on the rooftop. The view was incredible; you could see everything—our school, the playground, and even the guard rushing toward us in full Bollywood 'you-are-so-dead' mode.

By this time, word had spread faster than a school rumour. What started as a two-man mission had turned into a full-blown army. All eight of us had climbed up, united in our quest for rooftop immortality. All of us were standing there, admiring the view, feeling like kings of the world, waving to the students coming from their buses, when the unthinkable happened.

The guard reported us.

Panic hit like an earthquake. From legends on the rooftop, we turned into fugitives on the run. One shout from a staff member below, and suddenly, it was Dhoom 4. Everyone bolted for the stairs at lightning speed. Some of us jumped two steps at a time; some slid down the railing. Kumbhkaran tripped halfway but got up like a true warrior. By the time we reached the ground floor, we were sweating buckets and out of breath.

But, of course, not everyone made it out unscathed. A few unlucky souls were caught mid-escape and had to face the legendary wrath of the staff. We don't know what words were exchanged (or yelled), but their ears are probably still ringing.

As for the rest of us? We survived to tell the tale. Who needs speeches and snacks when you have rooftop adventures, the thrill of a guard chase, and a squad of eight partners in crime?

Farewell Not Fair

AFPI, mai tumhe ache se jaanti hu!
—Neha Ma'am, Shemrock

Hardly had we all left the Academy when something unexpected happened back at school—something that, in a way, made our departure even more memorable. The farewell planned for the whole batch was cancelled by the school because of the behaviour displayed by the juniors at the school. The juniors had themselves engaged in what I would write as an act of unity against another Academy, true to the AFPI spirit. But, at the end, seniors had to get involved, which became the final nail in the coffin of the farewell.

It was supposed to be the day we got our final school batch photograph clicked, a symbol of unity for the batch of 2024. But fate had other plans. Standing in line, uniforms crisp and spirits high, when we were all set for the photograph with our iconic 'Say *benzeeeeen*', a way of saying 'Smile please', the sounds of commotion from the direction of the buses changed everything.

'Something's happening with the juniors. Let's check it out,' one of my batchmates whispered sharply.

We broke formation and rushed toward the scene. The sight before us was infuriating—students from another Academy within the school were blocking our juniors from boarding their bus. While our juniors were trying to handle it, things were spiralling out of control.

Tensions rose. A heated exchange of words began between the academies. We, initially trying to calm down the situation, now spoke up because we were ready to digest anything but a mark of disrespect towards AFPI.

Before things could escalate further, the school authorities stepped in. While the other Academy kept on going, like animals in a forest, disrespecting the authorities present, we stepped back respectfully, just gracefully enough, to make sure that the others knew why we were AFPIans, and they were not. The juniors moved into their buses and headed back to the Academy while we took charge of the final situation.

When we returned to the Academy, we reported everything to IO Sir. 'Sir, they were disrespecting the AFPIan mark. We couldn't just stand by,' we explained.

He nodded, acknowledging our intentions. 'Discipline is important, but so is loyalty. You did what you thought was right.'

No matter how many mistakes we made or how badly we handled things at times, one truth always stood firm: the staff, the course, and AFPI always cared for us. It wasn't just about discipline; it was about ensuring we grew stronger, wiser, and better prepared for the road ahead. That day, like so many others, reminded me that being an AFPIan wasn't just a title—it was a responsibility, a bond, and a family.

◆◆◆

We put in our best efforts, determined to secure the farewell, but it felt like an uphill battle from the start. I first approached Seema Ma'am, who immediately told me that nothing could be done but suggested I try with Principal Ma'am. Knowing she had already turned down everyone else, I didn't expect much. But to my surprise,

Principal Ma'am agreed. The next hurdle was getting the Chairman's approval, but he swiftly denied our request. Despite the setback, my best friend, Anvita, an eleventh class student whom I met through editorial work on the school book, and I didn't give up. We approached the Chairman multiple times, and in the end, he gave his approval. Throughout all of this, Anvita never gave up. I remember one day when we were both exhausted and unsure of our next step but Anvita, despite the discouragement, said, 'We've come this far; we can't back down now.' Her words motivated me when I felt like giving up. At one point, we even made a bet with Neha Ma'am. 'We'll get the farewell, Ma'am. We're sure of it,' I said, grinning.

'Oh really?' Anvita added with a wink. 'We're basically the dream team.' Neha Ma'am chuckled. 'I'll take that bet. We'll see who wins.' In the end, we lost the bet. Neha Ma'am was right—her experience gave her the edge. But we didn't mind too much; we had given it our all. After all our efforts, just when it seemed we had a chance, one of the school committee members rejected the idea, and all our work went down the drain.

So here this was—the definite cancellation of the school farewell. It could have been disheartening, but the way the juniors at the Academy rallied around us, giving us a farewell that no one could have ever imagined, filled that void. They didn't let us feel the loss of that school farewell. Instead, they gave us a farewell at the Academy that will forever be etched in our hearts.

The farewell was a night to remember. It wasn't just a simple goodbye; it was a festival, a rollercoaster of emotions, laughter, and the wildest games and competitions. It was the night when legends were made and legacies were cemented. And, of course, it was the night when the juniors had their ultimate revenge on us—through titles. Oh, the titles they gave us! Some flattering, some questionable, and some downright hilarious.

Kirmada, our beloved troublemaker, walked away with the prestigious title of Mr Bakchod—his ability to turn even the most serious moments into pure chaos was simply in a league of its own. Then there was Mr AFPI, NSG, a title awarded to the guy who somehow managed to convince everyone he had the discipline of an elite commando, and for sure, he deserved it. Mr GOAT, naturally, went to our very own Bakra. And then there was Mr Chhupa Rustam, a.k.a. Husan, who had a quiet air about him but somehow managed to leave a trail of admirers wherever he went, and Mr Perfect went to the one and only Guruji for his utmost discipline and probably the only 24/7 clean room guy in the Academy.

But the highlight of the night? The one title that eclipsed all others? The ultimate crown jewel of the farewell: Mr Casanova. Now, this wasn't just handed out. Oh no, this title came with a competition. A fierce, no-holds-barred contest that tested not just charm but also influence, reputation, and, of course, sheer audacity.

And let me tell you, I was in the running. Oh yes, I was right there, fighting tooth and nail, thinking I had a shot. I mean, I had the charm, the skills, the smooth one-liners, and the runner-up factor written all over me. But then there was Sariya, the living Casanovic legend.

Let me paint a picture of why Sariya was declared the winner. You see, Sariya wasn't just a contender; he was a phenomenon. If there was a girl in school, chances were he was already talking to her before you even knew her name. If she had a best friend, he was bester friends with her best friend. If you dared to name a girl, Sariya not only had her number but probably had her Netflix password, too. His charm was omnipresent, his reach legendary. He was the guy who could casually say, 'Oh yeah, I know her,' about a girl you thought lived in a different continent.

But what truly sealed the deal? The girl Pujara liked. Now Pujara was someone we would call the polar opposite of a Casanova, with him getting three rapid 'NOs' from the girl in reply to 'Do you have Instagram, do you have Snapchat, and do you have any social media?' We now dared Sariya, always the smooth operator, to go and talk to the girl. What followed? Sariya swooped in like an eagle, approached her during the lunch break, and was seen sitting and chatting with the girl throughout the break while Pujara watched from the sidelines.

And then, it was official. Sariya, the one and only, was crowned Mr Casanova of the farewell. A legacy etched in stone.

The farewell wasn't just an event—it was a celebration, a spectacle, and a reminder that no matter how good you think you are, there's always a Sariya lurking around the corner. And that's the beauty of it. Legends like him don't just win titles—they redefine them.

◆◆◆

But life at the Academy was never just about studying and training—it was about those moments that would stay with us forever, both the good and the bad. Our final exams were coming up, but just after the farewell came chaos. The Titans were not willing to run the cross-country race for reasons as simple as lack of practice and exams coming up. The director, in his anger, threatened to throw us all out of the Academy. It was a dramatic moment because we were the ones to find fun in the heated moments, and one of us sarcastically exclaimed, 'Time to bid an early farewell to the Academy.'

◆◆◆

To make matters worse, we couldn't help but celebrate the traditional AFPIan style Holi, for which we hung a pair of shorts onto the camera.

Now, for this Holi, the Academy gifted us with a brand-new fire system. It was supposed to be a symbol of safety and modernisation. But for us? It became the ultimate source of fun during Holi as the fire system came with fire hoses installed with high water pressure on every floor in every block. But even this came with its own treasure of gold comedy.

One evening, as the guard was doing his routine rounds, Moan decided it was the perfect time to stir things up. With a completely innocent face and a tone of genuine curiosity, he approached the guard and said, 'Sir, we've seen a lot of fire exit signs around. But tell me one thing—these exits get locked at night, right? So, if there's a fire, do these doors magically unlock themselves? Or do we just burn inside?'

You could see the guard's brain short-circuiting in real time. His confident stride suddenly slowed down, and he looked at the doors like they had betrayed him. For a solid minute, he stood there, scratching his head, mumbling something about 'protocols' and 'safety systems'. The man was questioning not just the fire exits but his entire job description.

We couldn't hold it in. Watching him pace back and forth, looking at the doors like they were part of some elaborate conspiracy, was too much. And just when we thought he was done, he turned to Moan and said, '*Tussi sahi keh rahe ho, yaar... agar* fire *ho gayi, fir kya karenge?*'

The man looked genuinely concerned now. It was as if he could already hear the flames crackling in the distance and see us banging on the locked doors. We half-expected him to radio headquarters and demand an immediate safety drill.

Of course, we couldn't let it go. Someone chimed in with, 'Sir, *aur agar* system fail *ho gaya, toh kya aap khud* hammer *leke darwaze todoge?*' That did it. The guard, now visibly flustered, waved us off and muttered something about '*Kya pagal log hain yeh*.'

For days after, every time we passed those fire exits, someone would dramatically tug on the locked door and yell, 'Open sesame!' And every time we saw that guard, we'd give him a knowing look, silently reminding him of the time he almost rewrote fire safety laws because of a harmless joke from Moan.

Safety first, they said. But in the Academy, comedy always takes the lead.

But now, let's go back to the actual use of the fire system. If it couldn't be used for safety, let us use it for Holi! This was an epic item added to our Holi inventory.

◆◆◆

It was a peaceful night until it wasn't. The first knock came like the calm before a storm. I opened the door, and there they were—KG, Thakur, Baghdadi, and Rana—all armed with colours in their hands and mischief in their eyes.

'Guys, hold on! Let me at least close my door. I don't want my room ruined!' I pleaded like a man defending his last bastion. They let me close the door, but as soon as I stepped out, chaos erupted.

Colours flew everywhere; it wasn't just a festival of colours—it was a festival of madness. The noise was so loud that even the juniors in the 'B' Block woke up. And then came our masterstroke: someone spotted the newly installed fire nozzles. Within seconds, we were using them like we were firefighting each other. It was all fun and games until the noise hit an all-time high.

Enter The Guard. Oh, but this wasn't just any guard. This man was a cross between Usain Bolt and Sherlock Holmes. The moment he appeared, we scattered like cockroaches. I swear, the man was faster than us! We'd sprint up the stairs on one side, thinking we were clever, only to find him already waiting on the other side. It was as if he had been summoned by some divine power. We ran left; he was there. We ran right; he was already there. At one point, I genuinely considered whether this man was teleporting or if he had some supernatural GPS (Global Positioning System) locked onto us.

When we tried to escape into our rooms, the guard had a strategy of his own—he would lock us inside! Imagine seven of us crammed into Sal Sharma's room, whispering, 'Call someone to let us out!' But every time someone came to help, they'd end up getting locked, too. By the end of it, we were a train of locked-up cadets, and the guard was the conductor of our misery.

The grand finale came when he caught all eight of us in Sal Sharma's room. Sosa, Marcos, and I tried one last Hail Mary. We came up with the genius plan of creating a distraction on another floor, but alas, there was no one left to execute it—everyone was already locked up! Eventually, with no moves left, we surrendered.

The next morning, I went to the gate to pick up some goodies, praying I wouldn't see The Guard. But fate had other plans. He was there, sitting next to another guard, narrating the legendary Holi chase.

'These cadets don't just play Holi,' he grumbled. 'They turn the Academy into a jungle gym!'

Then, the other guard spotted me and said, 'Oh, not him! He's a *bhola-bhala* (innocent) guy. He doesn't do such things. Nahi *chittiyaa* (white man).'

I could barely contain my laughter as I nodded solemnly, doing my best to look innocent. Inside, though, I was dying. As I walked away, I thought, if only he knew....

That Holi night wasn't just a celebration—it turned into an adventure, a battle, and a comedy of errors all wrapped into one. As for the Guard? If there were ever an award for the quickest, most clever person on campus, he would definitely take the gold.

The official Holi celebrations the next day were cancelled. The director was furious, and though we apologised, punishment was inevitable. The juniors, who had followed our lead and recreated the chaos in their own blocks, were made to stand in the *savdhaan* position for three hours straight on the football ground, spaced six feet apart from one another. Strangely, nothing was said to us. Instead, we were told, 'You are just guests of the Academy now; you'll be leaving soon.' For a moment, it felt as though the Academy, once our home, was slipping away from us. The seniority and punishments we had once cherished now felt distant—like we were on the outside looking in.

Then came the cross-country. No choice, no practice. This event was a test of honour in itself for the course, and I, who had never left my running practice throughout the entire series of events, was the one carrying the hopes of the whole course. It was a battle, not just for me but for the pride of the course. I was told, 'Shivam, either you come first, or you don't come at all.' The pressure was immense. They wanted the Titan's name on the Hodson's Horse board, and it was a matter of honour.

I ran—faster than I ever had, pushed by a relentless need to prove something not just to myself but to my course, my brothers. A dog, which had somehow joined the race, chased me along as if urging me to keep going. I crossed the finish line in 16 minutes and 15 seconds. The second-place finisher, Sandhu, a junior, was 30 seconds behind. It felt like a win, but not just for me. It was a victory for the whole of Titans. It was our name, our pride, on that board.

My name is on the Hodson's board, though I never got a picture of it. I never saw the 598/A/12 while I was there, but for me, only the 12 mattered—it was my course, my legacy.

◆◆◆

And then came the POP.

The Passing Out Parade—the day that marked the end of our journey at the Academy. It should have been pure joy, but there was something so profoundly emotional about it. We had completed two years, but the thought of leaving behind everything we had fought for, the brothers we had become, made the day feel like both a win and a loss. We were to leave on April 21, the day of our second NDA attempt, and the POP would be the last day we'd walk those grounds as cadets. After that, we would be like guests in our own home.

The director, in his closing speech, said something that would stay with us forever: 'Believe you me, I know you backwards, better than your own parents and let me tell you, you all share the best bond I have ever seen. Never leave it behind and hold strong to it.' He was right. It wasn't just the training or the rules that defined us—it was the bond we had created, forged through countless challenges, late nights, laughter, and tears.

As we stood there, lined up for the final salute, the realisation hit us. This wasn't just the end of our time in the Academy; it was the beginning of something far greater. The friendships, the lessons, the struggles—all of it had prepared us for the real world. The director's words echoed in our minds: we were more than just a batch; we were brothers. And that bond would remain with us no matter where life took us.

As we made our way toward the flag, saluting the AFPI flag one last time, our juniors shouted, 'Twelfth course *ki Jai!* Seniors *ki Jai!*' The words filled the air, a powerful echo of tradition and respect. It felt like just yesterday that we had been standing where they were, reciting these very words for our own seniors, filled with the same pride and reverence.

At that moment, the circle of time felt complete. What we had once given, we were now receiving. One thing was certain: the legacy of the bond we had created would live on, forever woven into the fabric of the Academy. And no matter where life took us, we would always be a part of this place, this family, and this legacy.

In the end, the Academy wasn't just a place—it was our home. It was where we became who we were always meant to be. And though the gates were closing behind us, we knew we were leaving with something far more precious than any title or achievement: a bond that could never be broken.

46 Gentlemen

This is the best course I have ever seen!
—Maj Gen Chauhan, Director

Under the watchful gaze of the sun, we stood on April 21, a day we had all been anticipating and fearing in equal measure—the day we were leaving after giving our NDA examination, with the hope of success shining brightly ahead. One by one, we made our way out of the Academy, each of us leaving behind the place that had shaped us in ways we could never fully describe. The tears, the laughter, the pain, the triumphs—all of it came flooding back as we said our goodbyes.

I looked around, feeling the weight of it all. A few of us, like me, had come to realise that this wasn't just an end; it was the beginning of something far greater. Our time at AFPI was drawing to a close, but the bond we shared would endure forever.

As I was about to leave, something unexpected happened. Sardool Sir, one of the guards who had witnessed our journey from the very beginning, stood by with a nostalgic gaze, his eyes glistening with unspoken emotion. With a voice full of warmth and sincerity, he called out, 'Take my number, lads. Call me anytime you want to relive the memories of this Academy. I'll always be here for you, no matter where life takes you.'

His words struck me deeply, as though he was passing on a part of himself to us. The Academy had done more than teach us discipline and strength; it had created something much more precious—a family. And no matter where life would take us, this bond would always remain.

Earlier that week, my understudy had given me a Buddha statue, a symbol of calmness in the face of hardship. The AFPIan song echoed in my mind: 'No matter the hardships, no matter the pain, AFPIANs HAVE FUN, WE DANCE IN THE RAIN'. Those words were not just a saying—they were a way of life. AFPI had taught us to face everything, no matter how tough, with a smile and a sense of unity.

That night, my father arrived to pick me up. I was the last Titan to leave the Academy, and as I closed the door of my room, Room 32, one last time, a mark appeared on my hand, blood starting to trickle out. For a moment, it felt as though the Academy had left me a lasting gift—a love bite, something to forever remind me of everything I had earned there. And as I now look at that mark, I know I will never forget the journey that has shaped me, both physically and mentally.

When I reached the gate, it was just me standing there, much like my OD had done before, about to pass on the shoes to my understudy. I was the last Titan, and yet, there was no grand farewell, just a few familiar faces—my understudy, the warden, Nirbhik, Sandhu, Gursahib, and the guard. It was quiet, but the silence held more meaning than words could express.

As the warden left, he glanced at me one last time, his face a mask of silent respect. The guard, noticing I was still standing there, instructed three juniors to help me load my things into the car. I was being handed over the baton in a way. When everything was packed and settled in the car, I looked around at the familiar faces one last time. The Academy, the people who had become family, were behind me now. I looked at my home for one last time. I may enter this place again, but it would never be the same as it had been. Nothing that I become a part of in the future could rival the time I spent here.

I said goodbye to each of them, and then, in a moment of finality, I turned to Param, my understudy. On the last day, I knew I needed to pass on responsibilities. And then, we shared a man hug, and as a brother, I added, 'Param, we are AFPIans. And forever, we are brothers.' He added softly, 'Sir, you'll always have a piece of this home.' I passed a smile, one that carried happiness yet tinged with nostalgia.

I drove away that night, the Academy fading into the distance, but the memories never left. The experiences, the lessons, the bond—all of it stayed with me. And as I glanced at the rearview mirror, I realised one thing: this was not the end of my journey, but a new beginning.

Because once an AFPIan, always an AFPIan. And no matter where life took us, we would always be bound together, brothers forever.

'We are AFPIans. And forever, brothers.'

Some stories don't die; they forever live in our hearts. The chapters may end here, but the story of our forever bond has just begun. To the brotherhood, the camaraderie and to the unforgettable Titans, cheers!

Epilogue

On the first day of college, I walked into the classroom, carrying the invisible weight of my upbringing, unsure of how the world outside the Academy would see me. I approached my teacher, and his words stopped me in my tracks: 'Are you from an army background?' It wasn't a question—it was recognition. Somehow, without knowing my story, he could see the discipline etched into my being, the resilience in my stance, the spark of leadership I'd carried all my life.

As time went on, I began to see the difference in myself. My experiences, shaped by years of training and discipline, set me apart from others. The NCC (National Cadet Corps) gave me the CPL (Corporal) rank in my very first year—something not often seen in first-year cadets. But for me, it wasn't about the rank—it was about continuing the legacy I had inherited. As an army brat, I didn't just grow up in a home—I grew up in a tradition, one that taught me to lead, to endure, and never to turn my back on my brothers.

Even now, that legacy follows me. The hooter near my quarter in the cantonment is more than just a sound; it's a trigger, a bridge between the present and the past. Each time it blares, it pulls me back to my Academy days, jolting me awake to the echoes of '*Fall in! Warden* Sahab*! Koi pakda gaya!*' For those fleeting seconds, I'm no longer in my room—I'm back in the barracks, surrounded by my brothers, my family, my home.

And when the reality of the present settles in, there's only silence and the quiet ache of longing. The hooter carries more than a sound—it carries memories of the sweat, the struggle, the unshakable bond of brotherhood that shaped me. It carries the voices of my brothers, the laughter in stolen moments, the tears hidden behind stoic faces. It carries my home—a home I left behind but will never truly let go of.

Looking back, I realise that the Academy didn't just teach me discipline or resilience. It gave me a family, a purpose, and a lifelong bond with something greater than myself. And now, every step I take is with that legacy in my heart. To the reader, know this: the journey isn't easy. It will break you, bend you, and rebuild you in ways you never imagined. But it's worth it. Because in the end, you don't just carry memories—you carry a life, a brotherhood, and a story that will live forever.

This story is mine.

Acknowledgements

This book took longer than expected, as AFPI's beauty constantly inspired new ideas, leading to multiple revisions until the very end. I'm grateful to all who helped bring this story to life.

First and foremost, I extend my deepest gratitude to Director Sir, Maj Gen Ajay H Chauhan, VSM, for granting me the privilege to chronicle my experiences at the Academy. Your unwavering support made this story possible.

To my Mumma and Papa, no words can express my gratitude. Your steadfast love and sacrifices are the foundation of everything I've done and my greatest strength.

To the Titans, your camaraderie and encouragement have been a constant source of inspiration. This book would not have been possible without you.

Thanks to Ms Birinder, my English teacher, whose motherly support and guidance gave me the strength and motivation to write this book.

I am deeply indebted to Keshav Singla ('Singla' in the book) for his unparalleled design and editorial finesse.

Lastly, a heartfelt thanks to my Genie for always supporting me and to all readers who gave this work a try. I hope it inspires you, just as this place has inspired me.

Thank you all for being part of this journey and helping me bring this dream to life.

This book is my return gift to AFPI and its fraternity.

Maharaja Ranjit Singh AFPI – Legacy of Excellence (2011 to March 2024)

🏅 **Achievements at a Glance:**

- **Graduated Cadets:** 516
- **SSB Qualified:** 320
- **Joined Training Academies:** 253
- **Commissioned Officers:** 169

IN **Republic Day Parade Achievements:**

- **2020:** Capt Vijaypal Singh Sra (1st Course) – BMP Mounted Contingent
- **2023:** Capt Harshdeep Singh Sohi (3rd Course) – MECH INF Marching Contingent
- **2025:** Maj Bikramjit Singh (3rd Course) – JAK RIF Marching Contingent (Awarded Best Marching Unit)

⚔ **Gallantry Awardees:**

- **2021:** Capt Vishvadeep Singh (1st Course) – Sena Medal
- **2021:** Lt Jasmeet Singh Bamrah (3rd Course) – CDS Commendation

📚 **Esteemed Instructors at Premier Institutions:**

- Maj Danish Chadha (1st Course) – NDA Khadakwasla
- Capt Varinderpal Singh Bal (1st Course) – Armoured Corps Centre

- Capt Armaanjit Singh Dhaliwal (3rd Course) – CTW MCME

🏆 NDA Merit List Toppers:

- **NDA-133:** Capt Gurvansh Singh Gosal (2nd Course)
- **NDA-138:** Capt Shashank Sharma (5th Course)
- **NDA-153:** SCC Armaanpreet Singh (12th Course)

🌟 Notable Achievements:

- **2019:** Capt Parbhdeep Singh (1st Course) – 1st Rank, JAG Entry
- **2020:** ACA Harpreet Singh (1st Course) – Sword of Honour & Gold Medal (OTA Chennai)
- **2020:** Flying Officer Raghav Arora (6th Course) – Sword of Honour & Best in Flying (AFA)
- **2018:** Capt Gurvansh Singh Gosal (2nd Course) – Bronze Medal (IMA POP)
- **2021:** ACA Loveneet Singh (5th Course) – Bronze Medal (IMA POP)
- **2024:** Cadet Gurkirat Singh (8th Course) – 1st in Art Stream (NDA-147)

🏛 Distinguished Appointments:

- **2023:** Mr Rishabh Dixit (1st Course) – Judge, Judicial Courts Jabalpur
- **2023:** Mr Rishabh Bhola, IPS (1st Course) – ASP, Tarn Taran

Maharaja Ranjit Singh AFPI continues to forge leaders who inspire, achieve, and lead with honor.

Your Turn to Make History:

- **Name:** ______________________________

Your Dream/Aspiration:

____
____
____
____
____
____
____

The Achievement You Aim to Attain:

____
____
____
____
____
____
____
____
____
____

Maharaja Ranjit Singh AFPI continues to inspire future legends—let your name be the next in this legacy of honor and excellence.

Share Your Best AFPI Memory:

- **My Most Cherished Memory at AFPI:**

____
____
____
____
____
____
____
____
____

Maharaja Ranjit Singh AFPI continues to inspire future legends—let your name and memories become part of this lasting legacy.